High School

Talksheets

Fifty Creative Discussions for
High School Youth Groups

by

David Lynn

Edited by Wayne Rice

Illustrations by Corbin Hillam

ZondervanPublishingHouse
Grand Rapids, Michigan
A Division of HarperCollinsPublishers

Zondervan/Youth Specialties Books

Adventure Games
Amazing Tension Getters
Called to Care
The Complete Student Missions Handbook
Creative Socials and Special Events
Divorce Recovery for Teenagers
Feeding Your Forgotten Soul (Spiritual Growth for Youth Workers)
Get 'Em Talking
Good Clean Fun
Good Clean Fun, Volume 2
Great Games for 4th–6th Graders (Get 'Em Growing)
Great Ideas for Small Youth Groups
Greatest Skits on Earth
Greatest Skits on Earth, Volume 2
Growing Up in America
High School Ministry
High School TalkSheets
Holiday Ideas for Youth Groups (Revised Edition)
Hot Talks
Ideas for Social Action
Intensive Care: Helping Teenagers in Crisis
Junior High Ministry
Junior High TalkSheets
The Ministry of Nurture
On-Site: 40 On-Location Programs for Youth Groups
Option Plays
Organizing Your Youth Ministry
Play It! Great Games for Groups
Teaching the Bible Creatively
Teaching the Truth about Sex
Tension Getters
Tension Getters II
Unsung Heroes: How to Recruit and Train Volunteer Youth Workers
Up Close and Personal: How to Build Community in Your Youth Group
Youth Specialties Clip Art Book
Youth Specialties Clip Art Book, Volume 2

HIGH SCHOOL TALKSHEETS

Youth Specialties Books are published by
Zondervan Publishing House
Grand Rapids, Michigan 49530

Copyright © 1987 by Youth Specialties, Inc.

ISBN 0-310-20931-5

Edited by Wayne Rice
Designed by The Church Art Works
Illustrated by Corbin Hillam

Printed in the United States of America

99 00 01 02 03 04 /ML/ 29 28 27 26 25 24

High School

Talksheets

Table of Contents

TABLE OF CONTENTS (continued)

* * * * *

How to Use TalkSheets

You have in your possession a very valuable book. It contains fifty instant discussions for high school youth groups. Inside, you will find reproducible "TalkSheets" covering a wide variety of "hot topics", plus simple step-by-step instructions on how to use them. All you need for fifty thought-provoking meetings is this book and access to a copy machine.

TalkSheets are versatile and easy to use. They can be utilized in a group meeting, a Sunday School class or during Bible study. They can be used either in small or large groups of people. The discussions they instigate can be as brief as twenty minutes, or as long as interest remains and time allows. You can build an entire youth group meeting around a single TalkSheet, or you can use TalkSheets to supplement other materials and resources you might be using. The possibilities are endless.

TalkSheets are much more than just another type of curriculum or workbook. They invite excitement and involvement in discussing important issues and growth in faith. TalkSheets deal with key topics that young people want to talk about. With interesting activities, challenging questions and eye-catching graphics, TalkSheets will capture the attention of your audience and will help them think and learn. The more you use TalkSheets, the more your young people will look forward to them.

TalkSheets are Discussion Starters

While TalkSheets can be used as curriculum for your program, they are primarily designed to be used as discussion starters. Everyone knows the value of a good discussion in which young people are interacting with each other. When they are talking about a given subject, they are most likely thinking seriously about it and trying to understand it better. They are formulating and defending their points of view and making decisions and choices. Discussion helps truth rise to the surface thereby making it easier for young people to discover it for themselves. There is no better way to encourage learning than through discussion.

A common fear among youth group leaders reticent about leading a group of teenagers in discussion is "What if the kids in my group just sit there and refuse to participate?" It is because of this fear that many choose to show a movie or give a prepared lecture.

Usually, the reason young people fail to take part in a discussion is simple: they haven't had the time or the opportunity to organize their thoughts. Most high school students haven't yet developed the ability to "think on their feet" — to be able to present their ideas spontaneously and with confidence. They are afraid to speak for fear they might sound stupid.

TalkSheets remove this fear. They offer a chance to interact with the subject matter in an interesting, challenging and non-threatening way, *before* the actual discussion begins. Not only does this give them time to organize their thoughts and to write them down, but it also helps remove any anxiety they might feel. Most will actually look forward to sharing their answers and hearing others' responses to the same questions. They will be ready for a lively discussion.

A Step-by-step User's Guide

TalkSheets are very easy to use, but do require some preparation on your part. Follow these simple instructions and your TalkSheet discussion will be successful:

1 **Choose the right TalkSheet for your group.** Each TalkSheet deals with a different topic. The one you choose will have a lot to do with the needs and the maturity level of your group. It is not necessary (or recommended) to use the TalkSheets in the order in which they appear in this book.

2 **Try it yourself.** Once you have chosen a specific TalkSheet, answer the questions and do the activities yourself. Imagine your students participating. This "role playing" will give you first-hand knowledge of what you will be requiring of your young people. As you fill out the TalkSheet, think of additional questions, activities and scriptures.

3 **Read the Leader's Instructions (on the back of each TalkSheet).** Numerous tips and ideas for getting the most out of your discussion are contained in the Leader's Instructions. Add your own thoughts and ideas. Fill in the date and the name of the group in the top right-hand corner of the leader's page.

4 **Remove the TalkSheet from the book.** The pages are perforated along the left margins for easy removal. The information is easier to copy when removed. Before making copies, you might wish to "white out" (with liquid paper) the page number.

5 **Make enough copies for everyone.** Each student will need their own copy. This book makes the assumption that everyone has access to a copy machine but any method of duplicating will suffice. Only the student's side of the TalkSheet need be copied. The leader's material on the other side is just for you, the leader.

Keep in mind that you are able to make copies for your group because we have given you permission to do so. U.S. copyright laws haven't changed. It is still mandatory that you request permission from a publisher before making copies of other published material. It is illegal not to do so. Permission is given for you to make copies of this material for your group only, not for every youth group in your state. Thank you for your cooperation.

6 **Introduce the Topic.** In most cases, it is important to introduce, or "set up", the topic before you pass out the TalkSheets to your group. Any method will do as long as it is short and to the point. Be careful not to "overintroduce" the subject. Don't use an introduction that is too "preachy" or which resolves the issue before you get started. You want only to stimulate interest and instigate discussion. That is the primary purpose of the introduction.

The simplest way to introduce the topic is verbally. You can tell a story, share an experience, or describe a conflict having to do with the subject. You might ask a simple question, such as "What is the first thing you think of when you hear the word _____?" (whatever the topic is). After some have volunteered a few answers, you could reply "It sounds like we all have different ideas on the subject; let's investigate it a bit further. . .", or something similar. Then you distribute the TalkSheets, make certain everyone has a pen or pencil, and you're on your way.

Here are some ways of introducing any of the topics in this book, all of which, of course, should be pertinent:

1. Show a short film or video.
2. Read an interesting passage from a book or magazine article.
3. Play a popular record dealing with the theme.
4. Present a short skit or dramatic reading.
5. Play a simulation game or role play.
6. Present some current statistics, survey results, or read a recent newspaper article.
7. Use an "ice breaker", such as a humorous game. For example, if the topic is "Fun", play a game to begin the discussion. If the topic is "Success", consider a game whose players experience success or failure.

8. Use posters, slides, or any other audio-visual aids available to help concentrate focus.

There are, of course, many other possibilities. The introduction of the topic is left to your discretion and good judgment. You are limited only by your own creativity. Suggestions are offered with each TalkSheet, but they are not mandatory for success. Remember that the introduction is an integral part of each session. It helps set the tone and will influence the kinds of responses you receive. Don't "load" the introduction to the point that the "answer" is revealed and the students feel hesitant about sharing their own opinions.

7 Give students time to work on their TalkSheet. After your introduction of the topic, pass out a copy of the TalkSheet to each member of the group. They should also have a copy of the Bible, as well as writing implements. There are usually five or six activities on each TalkSheet. If time is limited, direct your students' interest to the specific part of the TalkSheet in which you wish them to participate.

Decide whether or not they should complete the TalkSheet on an individual basis or in groups.

Encourage your group to consider what the Bible has to say as they complete their TalkSheets.

Announce a time limit for their written work, then make them aware when one or two minutes remain. They may need more time, or less. Use your own judgment, depending upon your observations of the majority of the group. The discussion is now ready to begin.

8 Lead the discussion. In order for the TalkSheets to be used effectively, all members of your group need to be encouraged to participate. You must foster a climate that is conducive to discussion by communicating that each person's opinion is worthwhile and each has a responsibility to contribute to the rest of the group. A variety of opinions is necessary for these TalkSheets to have meaning.

If your group is large, you may want to divide it into smaller ones of six to twelve each. One person in each smaller group should be appointed facilitator to keep the discussion alive. The facilitator can be either an adult or another young person. Advise the leaders not to try and dominate the group, but to be on the same level with each member. If the group looks to the facilitator for the "answer", have the leader direct the questions or responses back to the group. Once the smaller groups have completed their discussion, have them reassemble into one large group, move through the items again and ask the different sections to summarize what they learned from each activity.

It is not necessary to divide up into groups every time TalkSheets are used. Variations provide more interest. You may prefer, at times, to have smaller groups of the same sex.

The discussion should center around the questions and answers on the TalkSheet. Go through them one at a time, asking volunteers to share how they responded to each item. Have them compare their answers and brainstorm new ones in addition to those they wrote down. Allow those who don't feel comfortable revealing their answers to remain silent.

Don't feel pressured to spend time on each activity. If time does not permit a discussion of every item, feel free to focus attention only on those provoking the higher interest.

Move with your own creative instinct. If you discover a better or different way to use the activity, do so. Don't feel restricted by the leader's instructions on the back of the TalkSheet. Use scriptures not found on the TalkSheet. Add your own items. TalkSheets were designed for you to be able to add your own thoughts and ideas.

If the group begins digressing into an area that has nothing to do with the topic, guide them back on track. However, if there is a high degree of interest in this "side issue", you may wish to allow the "extra" discussion. It may meet a need of many in the group, therefore would be worth pursuing.

More information on leading discussions is found on page 8.

Wrap up the discussion. This is your chance to challenge the group. When considering your closing remarks, ask yourself the following question: What do you want the group to remember from this experience? If you can answer in two or three sentences, then you have your closing remarks. It is important to bring some sort of closure to the session without negating the thoughts and opinions expressed by the group. A good "wrap-up" should affirm the group and offer a summary that helps tie the discussion together. Your students should be left with the desire to discuss the issue further, among themselves or with a leader. Tell your group members you are available to discuss the issue privately after the meeting. In some cases, a "wrap-up" may be unnecessary; just leave the issue hanging and bring it up again at a later date. This allows your students to wrestle with the issues on their own. Later, resolutions can evolve.

Follow-up with an additional activity. The leader's instructions on the back of the TalkSheet provide you with ideas for additional activities. They are optional but highly recommended. Their purpose is to afford an opportunity to reflect upon, evaluate, review and integrate what has been learned. Most of your TalkSheet discussions will generate a desire to discuss the subject matter again, which leads to better assimilation and more learning.

Assign the activity and follow-up on the assignment with a short, debriefing talk at the next group meeting. Appropriate questions about the activity would be:
1. What happened when you did this activity? Was it helpful or a waste of time?
2. How did you feel while you were doing the activity?
3. Did the activity change your mind or affect you in any way?
4. In one sentence, tell what you learned from this activity.

How to Lead a TalkSheet Discussion

The young people of today are growing up in a world of moral confusion. The problem facing youth workers in the church is not so much how to teach the church's doctrines but how to help them make the right choices when faced with so many options. The church's response to this problem has traditionally been to indoctrinate — to preach and yell its point of view louder than the rest of the world. This kind of approach does not work in today's world. Teenagers are hearing a variety of voices and messages, most of which are louder than those they hear from the church.

A TalkSheet discussion is effective for just this very reason. While discussing the questions and activities on the TalkSheet, your students will be encouraged to think carefully about issues, to compare their beliefs and values with others and will learn to make the right choices. TalkSheets will challenge your group to evaluate, defend, explain and rework their ideas in an atmosphere of acceptance, support and growth.

Characteristics of a TalkSheet Discussion

Remember, successful discussions — those that produce learning and growth — rarely happen by accident. They require careful preparation and sensitive leadership. Don't be concerned if you feel you lack experience at this time, or don't have the time to spend for a lengthy preparation. The more TalkSheet discussions you lead, the easier they will become and the more skilled you will be. It will help if you read the material on the next few pages and try to incorporate these ideas into your discussions.

The following suggestions will assist you in reaching a maximum level of success:

 Create a climate of acceptance. Most teenagers are afraid to express their opinions because they are fearful of what others might think. Peer approval is paramount with teenagers. They are fearful of being ridiculed or thought of as being "dumb". They need to feel secure before they share their feelings and beliefs. They also need to know they can share what they are thinking, no matter how unpopular or "wild" their ideas might be. If any of your students are submitted to put-downs, criticism, laughter or judgmental comments, especially if what they say is opposed to the teachings of the Bible or the church or their leader, an effective discussion will not be forthcoming.

For this reason, each TalkSheet begins with a question or activity less threatening and more fun than some of the questions that follow. The first question helps the individuals to become more comfortable with each other and with the idea of sharing their ideas more openly.

When asking a question, even one that is printed on the TalkSheet, phrase it to evoke *opinions*, not *answers*. In other words, if a question reads "What should Bill have done in that situation?", change it to "What *do you think* Bill should have done?" The addition of the three words "do you think" makes the question a matter of opinion rather than a matter of knowing the right answer. When young people realize their opinions are all that are necessary, they will be more apt to feel comfortable and confident.

2 **Affirm all legitimate expressions of opinion from your group members.** Let each person know their comments and contributions are appreciated and important. This is especially true for those who rarely participate. When they do, make a point of thanking them. This will encourage them and make them feel appreciated.

Keep in mind affirmation does not necessarily mean approval. Affirm even those comments that seem like "heresy" to you. By doing so, you let the group know everyone has the right to express their ideas, no matter what they are. If someone does express an opinion that you believe is "way off base" and needs to be corrected, make a mental note of the comment and present an alternative point of view in your concluding remarks, in a positive way. Do not attack or condemn the person who made the comment.

3 **Discourage the group from thinking of you as the "authority" on the subject.** Sometimes young people will think you have the "right answer" to every question and they will watch for your reaction, even when they are answering someone else's question. If you find the group's responses are slanted toward your approval, redirect them to the whole group. For example, you could say "Talk to the group, not to me" or "Tell everyone, not just me".

It is important for you to try to let them see you as a "facilitator" — another member of the group who is helping make the discussion happen. You are not sitting in judgment of their responses, nor do you have the right answer to every problem.

Remember, with teenagers, your opinions will carry more weight the less of an authority figure you appear to be. If you are regarded as an affirming friend, they will pay much more attention to what you have to say.

4 **Actively listen to each person.** God gave you one mouth and two ears. Good discussion leaders know how to listen. Your job is not to monopolize the discussion, or to contribute the wisest words on each issue. Keep your mouth shut except when you are encouraging others to talk. You are a facilitator. You can express your opinions during your concluding remarks.

5 **Do not force anyone to talk.** Invite people to speak out, but don't attempt to force them to do so. Each member should have the right to "pass".

6 **Do not take sides during the discussion.** Hopefully, you will have disagreements in your group from time to time and students who will take opposing viewpoints. Don't make the mistake of siding with one group or the other. Encourage both sides to think through their positions and to defend their points of view. You might ask probing questions of both, to encourage deeper introspection of all ideas. If everyone seems to agree on a question, or if they seem fearful of expressing a controversial point, it might be beneficial for you to play "devil's advocate" with some thought-provoking comments. This will force them to think. Do not give them the impression that the "other" point of view is necessarily your own, however. Remain neutral.

7 **Do not allow one person (including yourself) to monopolize the discussion.** Almost every group has that "one person" who likes to talk and is perfectly willing to express their opinion on every question. Try to encourage everyone to participate.

8 **Arrange seating to encourage discussion.** "Theater style" seating, i.e. in rows, is not conducive to conversation. If you must use chairs at all, arrange them in a circular or semi-circular pattern.

Occasionally, smaller groups of four or six are less threatening to teenagers, especially if there is a variety of maturity levels in the group. If you have both junior high level and senior high level in the same group, it might be preferable to segregate them accordingly.

9 **Allow for humor when appropriate.** Do not take the discussion so seriously as to prohibit humor. Most TalkSheets include questions that will generate laughter as well as some intense dialogue.

10 **Don't be afraid of silence.** Many discussion leaders are intimidated by silence in the group. Their first reaction is to fill the silence with a question or a comment. The following suggestions may help you handle silence more effectively:

a. Learn to feel comfortable with silence. Wait it out for thirty seconds. Give someone a reasonable time to volunteer a response. If you feel it appropriate, invite a specific person to talk. Sometimes a gentle nudge is all that is necessary.

b. Discuss the silence with the group. Ask them what the silence really means. Perhaps they are confused or embarrassed and don't feel free to share their thoughts.

c. Answer the silence with questions or comments about it. Occasionally, comments such as "It's a difficult issue to consider, isn't it?" or "It's scary to be the first to talk" may break the ice.

d. Ask a different question that might be easier to handle or that might clarify the one that has been proposed. But don't do this too quickly. Wait a short while, first.

11 **Try to keep the discussion under control.** Frequently a discussion can become sidetracked onto a subject you may not consider desirable. If someone brings up a side issue that generates a lot of interest, you will need to decide whether or not to pursue that issue and see where it leads or redirect the conversation back to the original subject. Sometimes it's a good idea to digress — especially if the interest is high and the issue worth discussing. In most cases, however, it is advisable to say something like "Let's come back to that subject a little later, if we have time. Right now, let's finish our discussion on. . .".

12 **Be creative and flexible.** Don't feel compelled to ask every question on the TalkSheet, one by one, in order. If you wish, ask only a couple of them, or add a few of your own. The leader's guide may give you some ideas, but think of your own as well. Each question or activity may lead to several others along the same lines, which you can ask during the discussion.

13 **Be an "askable" discussion leader.** Make certain your young people understand they can talk to you about anything and find concern and support, even after the TalkSheet discussion has been completed.

14 **Know what your goals are.** A TalkSheet discussion should be more than just a "bull session". TalkSheets are designed to move the conversation toward a goal, but you will need to identify that goal in advance. What would you like the young people to learn? What truth would you like them to discover? What is the goal of the session? If you don't know where you are going, it is doubtful you will arrive.

Ground Rules for an Effective TalkSheet Discussion

A few ground rules will be helpful before beginning your TalkSheet discussions. Rules should be kept to a minimum, but most of the time young people will respond in a positive manner if they know in advance what is expected of them. The following are suggestions for you to consider using:

1 **"What is said in this room stays in this room."**

Confidentiality is vitally important to a healthy discussion. The only time it should be broken is if a group member reveals he/she is going to do harm to themselves or another person.

2 **"No put-downs".**

Mutual respect is important. If someone disagrees with another's comment, they should raise their hand and express an opinion of the comment, but not of the person who made it. It is permissable to attack ideas, but not each other.

3 **"There is no such thing as a dumb question".**

Your youth and adult leaders must feel free to ask questions at any time. Asking questions is the best way to learn.

4 **"No one is forced to talk".**

Let everyone know they have the right to remain silent about any question.

5 **"Only one person talks at a time".**

This is one way to teach young people mutual respect. Each person's opinion is worthwhile and deserves to be heard.

If members of the group violate these rules during the discussion or engage in disruptive or negative behavior, it would be wise to stop and deal with the problem before continuing.

Using the Bible with TalkSheets

Adults often begin discussions with younger people assuming they believe the Bible has authority over their lives. Adults either begin their discussions with scripture or quickly support their contentions with Bible verses. Young people of today often consider their life situations first, then decide if the Bible fits. TalkSheets are designed to deliberately begin your discussion with the realities of the adolescent world and then move toward scripture. This gives you the opportunity to show them the Bible can be their guide and that God does have something to say that is applicable to their age level and their interests.

The last activity on each TalkSheet involves scripture. These Bible references were selected for their relevance to each issue and for their potential to generate healthy discussion. They are not to be considered exclusive. It is assumed you will add whatever scriptures you believe are equally pertinent. The passages listed are only the tip of the iceberg, inviting you to "search the scriptures" for more.

Once the scriptures have been read aloud, invite your group to develop a Biblical principle that can guide their lives. For example, after reading the passages on the topic of "Fun" (Kids Just Want to Have Fun), the group may summarize thusly: "God wants us to have fun that is not harmful to us. It is best to include God in all the fun we have."

A Word of Caution. . .

Many of the TalkSheets in this book deal with topics which may be sensitive or controversial. Discussing subjects such as sexuality or even materialism may not be appreciated by everyone in the church. Whenever you encourage discussion on such topics, or encourage young people to express their opinions (on any subject) no matter how "off base" they may be, you risk the possibility of criticism from parents or other concerned adults in your church. They may believe you are teaching the youth group heresy or questionable values.

The best way to avoid problems is to use good judgment. If you have reason to believe a particular TalkSheet is going to cause problems, it would be judicious to think twice before you use it. Sometimes the damage done by going ahead outweighs the potential good.

Another way to avoid misunderstandings is to provide parents and others to whom you are accountable copies of the TalkSheet before you use it. Let them know what you hope to accomplish and the type of discussion you will be encouraging.

It would also be wise to suggest your young people take their TalkSheet home and discuss it with their parents. They might want to ask their parents how they would answer some of the questions.

I WISH I WERE DEAD

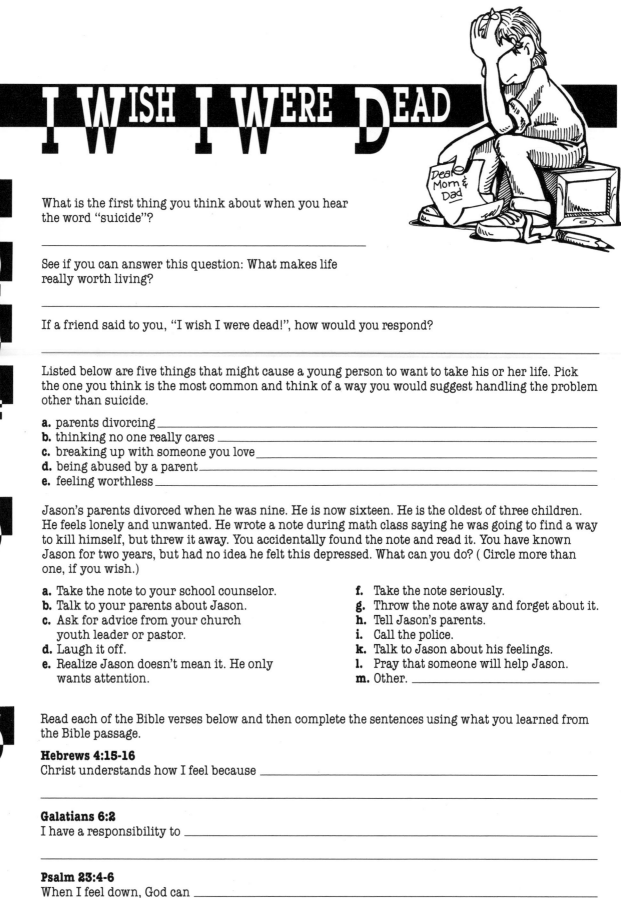

1 What is the first thing you think about when you hear the word "suicide"?

_____

2 See if you can answer this question: What makes life really worth living?

_____

3 If a friend said to you, "I wish I were dead!", how would you respond?

_____

4 Listed below are five things that might cause a young person to want to take his or her life. Pick the one you think is the most common and think of a way you would suggest handling the problem other than suicide.

a. parents divorcing _____
b. thinking no one really cares _____
c. breaking up with someone you love _____
d. being abused by a parent _____
e. feeling worthless _____

5 Jason's parents divorced when he was nine. He is now sixteen. He is the oldest of three children. He feels lonely and unwanted. He wrote a note during math class saying he was going to find a way to kill himself, but threw it away. You accidentally found the note and read it. You have known Jason for two years, but had no idea he felt this depressed. What can you do? (Circle more than one, if you wish.)

a. Take the note to your school counselor.
b. Talk to your parents about Jason.
c. Ask for advice from your church youth leader or pastor.
d. Laugh it off.
e. Realize Jason doesn't mean it. He only wants attention.

f. Take the note seriously.
g. Throw the note away and forget about it.
h. Tell Jason's parents.
i. Call the police.
k. Talk to Jason about his feelings.
l. Pray that someone will help Jason.
m. Other. _____

6 Read each of the Bible verses below and then complete the sentences using what you learned from the Bible passage.

Hebrews 4:15-16
Christ understands how I feel because _____

_____

Galatians 6:2
I have a responsibility to _____

_____

Psalm 23:4-6
When I feel down, God can _____

_____

I WISH I WERE DEAD

Topic: Suicide

Purpose of this Session:

This TalkSheet gives your group the chance to explore the topic of suicide. Allowing young people to talk about suicide has several benefits: (1) Talking helps them share their feelings if they have had a friend or relative who has committed suicide. (2) Talking helps them uncover their own fears of suicide and death. (3) Talking about suicide can help your group realize they can, as Christians, show their love to other young people who are hurting.

To Introduce the Session:

Too often, the news media of today's world features the tragedy of teenage suicides. It is possible that some of your teenagers know someone who committed suicide. You might begin this session by reading one of these news articles to the group.

The Discussion:

Item #1: If your group is having difficulty using the word 'suicide' or talking about it, have them say the word together aloud. Allow them to share their feelings about suicide. Be careful and sensitive to the fact that some of them may have known and loved a person who has committed suicide. Your young people need to share all kinds of emotional responses, from guilt and self-blame to anger and resentment. Take the time to talk about each of these reactions.

Item #2: A person's basic philosophy of life is summarized in their answer to this question. You can learn a great deal about each of your students and their beliefs from their response.

Item #3: Encourage your group to share their answers. Move the group to a point where they recognize the need to encourage this friend to seek professional help if indeed he or she is considering suicide. Tell your students they should *always* take remarks, and thoughts, about suicide *seriously*.

This question would be effective as a role playing device. Have one person pretend to be the person who is considering suicide. Have another pretend to be the friend listening as the first one says "I wish I were dead". Permit the conversation to continue for two or three minutes, then let another pair try it.

Item #4: Discuss these five "reasons for suicide" one at a time, asking the students to tell you all the alternatives they were able to think of. Ask them to evaluate each idea as to its effectiveness, practicality, etc. It is important they understand there are lots of other options available.

Item #5: Use this "Tension Getter" to talk about ways Christians should respond to a hurting person. Responses a, b, c, f, h, i and k would be appropriate. Some in your group may think of additional reactions. Have the rest of the students discuss them, too.

Item #6: Ask your students to share their completed sentences with the rest of the group. Stress our responsibility as Christians to support and encourage others, even those not in our group or clique.

To Close the Session:

Focus on Hebrews 4:15-16, stressing Christ's understanding of our every problem. Challenge them to bring their problems and feelings to Christ and to the church, even though they may feel God is far away. Help them to see things are never as bad as they seem. Tell them when we know Christ, we can be confident even the bad things in life will "work together for our good" (Romans 8:28). Christ has come to give us "abundant life" (John 10:10) and He will if we will allow Him to.

You may want to close with some suggestions about recognizing someone who is seriously in danger of taking his or her own life. There are a number of books and other resources available which provide this information. If there is a suicide "hotline" in your area, post the number for the students to write down. You might also suggest the names of adult counselors in your church or in the immediate vicinity who are qualified to provide help to potential suicide victims.

Additional Activity:

Ask each person to write a letter to a fictional "friend" their age, whom they suspect is seriously considering suicide. Allow time for them to share these letters in small discussion groups. Emphasize the importance of sharing Christian faith in the letters.

THE DATING GAME

1 Describe a "perfect 10" date.

_____
_____
_____
_____

2 I would like to date a person who: (check three)

_____ can be open and honest with me.
_____ treats me as if I am special and with respect.
_____ will listen when I need to talk.
_____ is popular.
_____ won't date anyone else but me.
_____ is very good-looking.

_____ likes to try new and different things.
_____ is very intelligent and gets good grades.
_____ is involved in church activities.
_____ wants to "get physical" right away.
_____ has a lot of money.
_____ is a strong Christian.
_____ has a sense of humor.

3 List four or five things to do on a date that are inexpensive and fun. _____

_____
_____
_____
_____

4 What do you think?

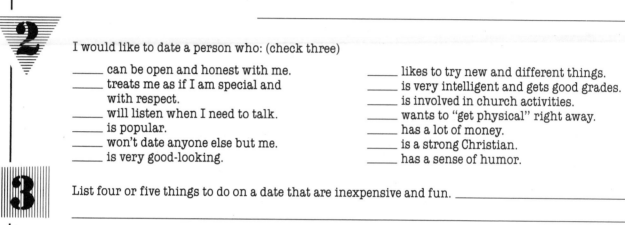

	YES	DEFINITELY	SOMETIMES	NEVER
a. A person should date as many people as he/she can.	—	—	—	—
b. Christians should pray together on a date.	—	—	—	—
c. The best age to begin dating is 14.	—	—	—	—
d. Heavy petting is okay as long as the couple doesn't go all the way.	—	—	—	—
e. Christians should date only other Christians.	—	—	—	—

	YES	DEFINITELY	SOMETIMES	NEVER
f. It's permissable for a girl to ask a guy for a date.	—	—	—	—
g. The purpose of dating is to prepare for marriage.	—	—	—	—
h. If your parents don't approve of the person you are dating, you should stop seeing her/him.	—	—	—	—
i. Couples should share expenses on a date.	—	—	—	—

5 Read the following scripture verses and write out what you think each verse has to say about dating.

I Kings 11:1-4 _____

I Corinthians 5: 9-11 _____

Galatians 5:16 _____

THE DATING GAME

Topic: Dating and the Christian

Purpose of this Session:

This TalkSheet will provide you with a forum for discussing dating. Unfortunately, peer pressure has increased tremendously toward dating at younger and younger ages. What does this mean for the Christian young person?

To Introduce the Session:

A humorous way to begin is to relate the following joke about yourself or one of your male associates:

"A friend of mine offered to get me a 'blind date' when I was in high school and I said there was no way. I told him the last time I had a blind date, she looked like ten miles of bad road. My friend suggested I go to her house, knock on the door, and if she wasn't up to par, just fake an asthma attack by wheezing and snorting loudly. Then I could turn around and leave. I thought it over and decided to try it. On the night of the big date, I arrived at the girl's house, knocked on the door and when she opened it, she doubled over with wheezes and snorts!"

Another introduction to this session is to have them form smaller groups for a skit. Tell them the theme is "dating" and let them create their own situation. They may want to act out a "first date", "boy meets girl", "the first kiss", etc. Debrief the skits when all have performed. Talk with them about what they have learned, both positive and negative, from the skits.

The Discussion:

Item #1: Some of the ideas this generates will be ridiculous and others will be worthwhile. List them visibly, in case you wish to refer to them later.

Item #2: This forces the students to assess their priorities and their values, because they are limited to three choices. In this manner, the most important traits will become evident. After a few volunteers share their choices, tally up the "votes" for each one and discover what the majority considers most important.

Item #3: This should evoke lots of ideas. Write all of the contributions down, making certain the students realize a "date" doesn't have to necessarily "look like" a date. Grocery shopping, puddle-jumping, a tour of a tennis-ball factory — anything wholesome and fun is acceptable. They will be surprised at the many ideas. You may want to make copies of all the suggestions for each of them.

Item #4: Discuss the statements they do not all agree on. If there is one that causes a lot of argument, let them debate the issue. Divide them into dissenting groups and give them time to formulate a "case" for their position before they begin. Encourage them to use Biblical support for their opinions.

Item #5: Dating is not mentioned in the Bible, specifically, so this exercise will give them the opportunity to apply scripture to modern day situations. After they share their interpretations, choose one of the passages you would like to focus on.

To Close the Session:

Reassure the students there is nothing abnormal about *not* dating. The dating game American young people play puts them under a great deal of pressure. Challenge them to encourge "group dating", without pairing off. Emphasize dating doesn't have to be "romantic"; instead, it can be just for healthy fun. Encourage them to plan an event that includes several friends, not just one.

Outside Activities:

Suggest that all or some of the students plan a group date with no pairing off and report back to the meeting afterward. Emphasize a group date is not a double date, but several of each sex going out in a group, getting to know each other better and having fun.

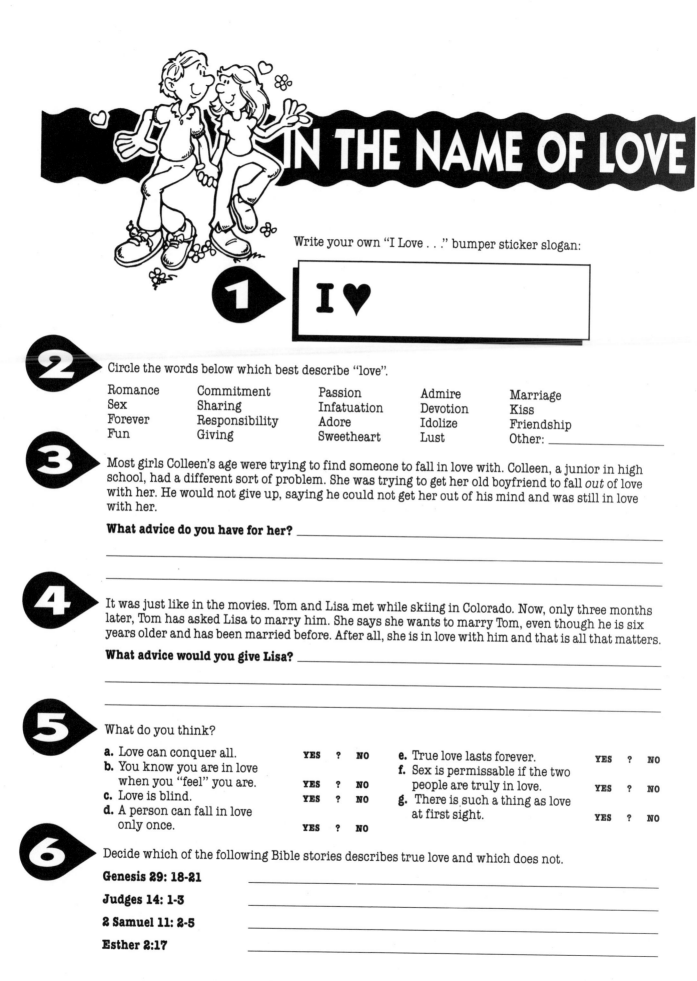

IN THE NAME OF LOVE

Write your own "I Love . . ." bumper sticker slogan:

1 I ♥

2 Circle the words below which best describe "love".

Romance   Commitment   Passion   Admire   Marriage
Sex   Sharing   Infatuation   Devotion   Kiss
Forever   Responsibility   Adore   Idolize   Friendship
Fun   Giving   Sweetheart   Lust   Other: _____

3 Most girls Colleen's age were trying to find someone to fall in love with. Colleen, a junior in high school, had a different sort of problem. She was trying to get her old boyfriend to fall *out* of love with her. He would not give up, saying he could not get her out of his mind and was still in love with her.

What advice do you have for her? _____

_____

_____

4 It was just like in the movies. Tom and Lisa met while skiing in Colorado. Now, only three months later, Tom has asked Lisa to marry him. She says she wants to marry Tom, even though he is six years older and has been married before. After all, she is in love with him and that is all that matters.

What advice would you give Lisa? _____

_____

_____

5 What do you think?

a. Love can conquer all.   YES ? NO
b. You know you are in love when you "feel" you are.   YES ? NO
c. Love is blind.   YES ? NO
d. A person can fall in love only once.   YES ? NO

e. True love lasts forever.   YES ? NO
f. Sex is permissable if the two people are truly in love.   YES ? NO
g. There is such a thing as love at first sight.   YES ? NO

6 Decide which of the following Bible stories describes true love and which does not.

Genesis 29: 18-21 _____

Judges 14: 1-3 _____

2 Samuel 11: 2-5 _____

Esther 2:17 _____

Date Used: _____

Group: _____

IN THE NAME OF LOVE

Topic: Romantic Love

Purpose of this Session:
Romantic love is a popular notion among young people and is being pushed heavily by the media. The purpose of this TalkSheet is to discuss what love really means. Many young people think love is merely a feeling that one gets when with a special someone. Jesus taught and lived a life of love that was more than a feeling. It was an action and a way of life.

To Introduce the Topic:
Separate the students into groups of three to six and have them prepare an original skit on love. Suggest only titles, such as "Love at First Sight", "First Love" or "Falling in Love".

The Discussion:
Item #1: Have each person read their "I LOVE. . ." bumper sticker. This should produce some humor and some insights into what is dear to them.

Item #2: After sharing everyone's choices, make a visible list of the favorites to refer to later. Remain neutral at this time and don't judge the words they have chosen. Ask why they have chosen the ones they did. Note how many agree.

Items #3 and #4: These "Tension Getters" offer an opportunity to discuss "true love" versus *feelings* of love, or "being *in* love". You may wish to discuss them from different angles. For example, in the first, suppose Colleen was not a Christian, or was pregnant, or had fallen in love with another guy. In the second, perhaps you could suppose Lisa is only sixteen, or that both Tom and Lisa are Christians. Would this make any difference?

Another idea is to divide the students into smaller groups, giving each one of these situations. Let them decide what should be done and then discuss their conclusions with the entire group.

Item #5: This should provoke a healthy discussion. Talk over each statement, digressing as much as time and interest permit. Let the subjects be debated. Some of the items may bring up the subject of divorce. Remember to be sensitive when discussing this issue. Several in the group will undoubtedly have divorced parents.

Item #6: Allow the kids to reflect on each of these Old Testament stories, and to share their opinions of them. Point out that not all Biblical characters were perfect.

To Close the Session:
Focus on and discuss the three kinds of love the Greeks described: *agape, phileo* and *eros*. Agape is God's love for us, a genuine, sacrificial love that is unselfish and giving. Phileo is friendship love. Eros is love on a more physical, sexual level. Concentrate on the love Christ exemplified.

Emphasize Christian love is much more than a feeling of infatuation or romance. It involves responsibility and commitment. It is decision, an act of the will. It always thrives best when the Author of love is included. Love is like a triangle (use the diagram below) with two people at the bottom and God at the top, or the apex. The closer the two people get to God, the closer they become to each other.

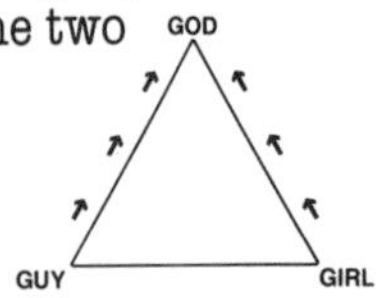

Outside Activities:
1. Ask the students to think of a song that describes love and critique the song. Allow them enough time to form opinions of the verses. Perhaps they can bring copies of the words to the session.

2. Give the group an opportunity to experience agape love through a service project that helps others.

3. Ask them to make posters describing the different kinds of love. Hang the posters in the meeting room and discuss them.

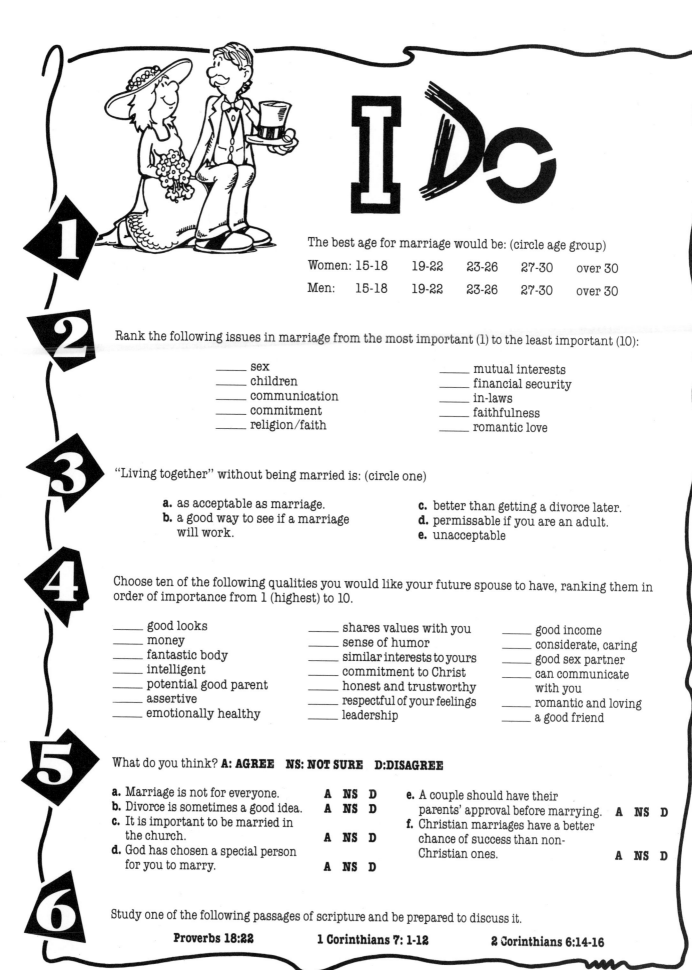

I DO

1

The best age for marriage would be: (circle age group)

Women: 15-18   19-22   23-26   27-30   over 30

Men: 15-18   19-22   23-26   27-30   over 30

2

Rank the following issues in marriage from the most important (1) to the least important (10):

_____ sex
_____ children
_____ communication
_____ commitment
_____ religion/faith

_____ mutual interests
_____ financial security
_____ in-laws
_____ faithfulness
_____ romantic love

3

"Living together" without being married is: (circle one)

a. as acceptable as marriage.
b. a good way to see if a marriage will work.

c. better than getting a divorce later.
d. permissable if you are an adult.
e. unacceptable

4

Choose ten of the following qualities you would like your future spouse to have, ranking them in order of importance from 1 (highest) to 10.

_____ good looks
_____ money
_____ fantastic body
_____ intelligent
_____ potential good parent
_____ assertive
_____ emotionally healthy

_____ shares values with you
_____ sense of humor
_____ similar interests to yours
_____ commitment to Christ
_____ honest and trustworthy
_____ respectful of your feelings
_____ leadership

_____ good income
_____ considerate, caring
_____ good sex partner
_____ can communicate with you
_____ romantic and loving
_____ a good friend

5

What do you think? **A: AGREE   NS: NOT SURE   D:DISAGREE**

a. Marriage is not for everyone.　　　　**A NS D**
b. Divorce is sometimes a good idea.　　**A NS D**
c. It is important to be married in the church.　　**A NS D**
d. God has chosen a special person for you to marry.　　**A NS D**

e. A couple should have their parents' approval before marrying.　　**A NS D**
f. Christian marriages have a better chance of success than non-Christian ones.　　**A NS D**

6

Study one of the following passages of scripture and be prepared to discuss it.

Proverbs 18:22　　　　**1 Corinthians 7: 1-12**　　　　**2 Corinthians 6:14-16**

Date Used: _____

Group: _____

I DO

Topic: Marriage

Purpose of this Discussion:

The divorce rate is high. Marriage problems abound. More and more couples live together without getting married. Perhaps some of the problems related to marriage could be avoided, if our young people could examine marriage within a Christian context and from a Christian perspective. This TalkSheet gives your group the opportunity to discuss in detail the institution of marriage.

To Introduce the Session:

Play a guessing game, the students sitting in a circle with a volunteer who is "it" sitting in the middle. On a piece of paper, each person writes their answer to the following questions:

1. Do you plan to be married someday?
2. At what age do you think you will get married?
3. Describe your idea of the person you want to marry.
4. How many children would you like to have?

The students try to guess how the person who is "it" answered the questions. Another suggestion is to invite a married couple and/or someone who is divorced to the meeting to discuss their experiences with marriage.

The Discussion:

Item #1: Opinions may very greatly. Let everyone tell their choices.

Item #2: Discuss the three most and the three least chosen by the majority. If possible, separate the group accordingly and let them debate the points.

Item #3: This is a vital subject to discuss openly because the practice of living together without being married is prevalent in our society. Divorce has affected many young people adversely and they harbor a fear of marriage as a result. Debate the pros and cons of living together. Try to get them to give their honest opinions. Save yours — and Biblical beliefs — for the closing statement.

Item #4: There should be a variety of choices with this exercise. Allow them to debate with each other several of their preferred traits. You may want to make a master list of the favorites and discuss them further.

Item #5: As you discuss these issues, be aware of the necessity for being sensitive to those who may have parents with marital problems. Permit those who are hurting, or who are helping others with family problems, to share their grief.

Item #6: Ask which passage they would most like to discuss first. Focus your attention on that choice. If time allows, move to the other two passages.

To Close the Session:

Share a brief Biblical view of marriage. Help your students see that despite the failure of many of today's marriages, it is a holy state and instituted by God. It should not be taken lightly. Marriage is one of the most important of life's decisions and with God's help, a marriage can be successful. For those who have experienced the pain of divorce, encourage them to be forgiving and turn their problems over to Christ. Remember to let them know you are available for private discussions.

Outside Activities:

1. Ask everyone to write a simulated Want Ad for a marriage partner. Read all the ads aloud and sum up what was learned.

2. Ask them to critique a television sit-com marriage for its good and bad points. Discuss their conclusions.

Struggling

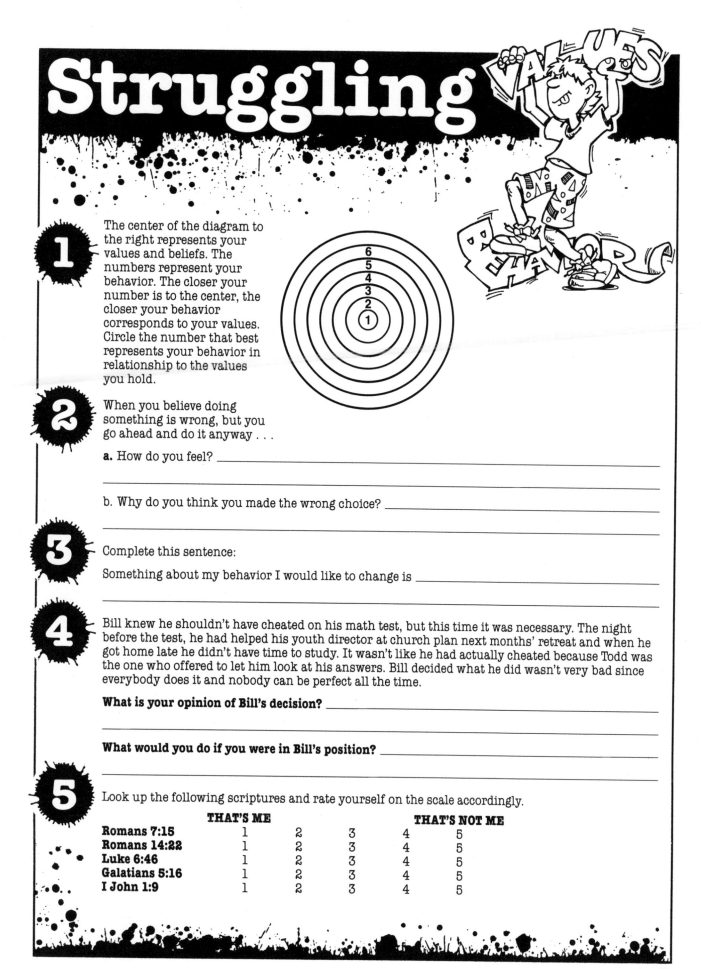

1 The center of the diagram to the right represents your values and beliefs. The numbers represent your behavior. The closer your number is to the center, the closer your behavior corresponds to your values. Circle the number that best represents your behavior in relationship to the values you hold.

2 When you believe doing something is wrong, but you go ahead and do it anyway . . .

a. How do you feel? _____

_____

b. Why do you think you made the wrong choice? _____

_____

3 Complete this sentence:

Something about my behavior I would like to change is _____

_____

4 Bill knew he shouldn't have cheated on his math test, but this time it was necessary. The night before the test, he had helped his youth director at church plan next months' retreat and when he got home late he didn't have time to study. It wasn't like he had actually cheated because Todd was the one who offered to let him look at his answers. Bill decided what he did wasn't very bad since everybody does it and nobody can be perfect all the time.

What is your opinion of Bill's decision? _____

_____

What would you do if you were in Bill's position? _____

_____

5 Look up the following scriptures and rate yourself on the scale accordingly.

	THAT'S ME			THAT'S NOT ME	
Romans 7:15	1	2	3	4	5
Romans 14:22	1	2	3	4	5
Luke 6:46	1	2	3	4	5
Galatians 5:16	1	2	3	4	5
I John 1:9	1	2	3	4	5

Date Used: _____

Group: _____

STRUGGLING

Topic: Values and behavior.

Purpose of this Session:

The teen years is the time in life when there usually occurs a great inconsistency between belief and behavior. This TalkSheet is stuctured to help you discuss the struggles faced as your students try to live by their standards of value. This discussion should only be proposed to young people who feel comfortable with and respect each other, as it requires a deep level of sharing and openness.

To Introduce the Topic:

Have the members play "tug of war". A rope is not necessary if the boys sit in a circle with their arms and legs locked together and then the girls try to pull them apart. Follow up the game with the comment, "Trying to live within our belief system is a lot like a tug of war. It's a real struggle — as if you were being pulled in two directions. That's what our discussion will be about." After the introduction, pass out the *STRUGGLING* TalkSheet.

The Discussion:

Item #1: Ask the students to write down (anonymously) the number they chose on a small slip of paper and pass it to you. Embarrassment, if any, is thereby avoided when you read the numbers off. Explain to the group that the longer a person's behavior is inconsistent with his beliefs, the more likely his beliefs will change to match his behavior.

Suggest specific values or beliefs for the center of the chart, such as "All men are created equal" or "It is more blessed to give than to receive". Ask them to share how their behavior matches up with these values.

Item #2: The students may describe feelings of guilt in answer to this exercise. Make certain they understand that guilt is not always "bad" — it was designed by God to pull our behavior patterns in line with our value system. When we stop feeling guilty for the inconsistency in our lives, then we are in serious trouble.

Item #3: If sharing the sentences is uncomfortable, pass out 3x5 cards and have them write their responses, passing them to you. Read them aloud and discuss them. Brainstorm practical ways to change incompatible behavior patterns.

Item #4: Discuss this "Tension Getter". Ask the group to rate Bill's actions on a scale of 1 to 10 (10 being good). Most will chose a middle-of-the scale number. Point out that life rarely is divided into nice, safe categories in which all our choices are obvious and easy to make, like a simple one or a ten. Sometimes they fall in the middle, in a grey area, not clearly black or white. We are all a mixture of good and bad, struggling in the grey area most of our lives. The important thing is to make the best decision we can and attempt to live out what we believe to the best of our ability. This cannot be achieved by rationalizing, as Bill may have done. Ask them to describe similar situations they have experienced and what they did in each case.

Item #5: Have the group look up each passage and allow the kids to evaluate where they stand on each one. If kids feel that they fall short of what God wants, help them to see that even a little improvement over time is better than no improvement at all.

To Close the Session:

Encourage your students to think through their values and then try to live consistently with them. They need to "walk their talk". You might choose a value everyone respects, such as "Christians should love their neighbors", and brainstorm a list of pertinent actions to be completed during the next week. Find methods to put good values into practice with consistency. The more frequently the right choices are made, the easier becomes the struggle.

Encourage the use of scripture for help and guidance. Suggest that they ask parents and other Christians when they are having difficulty making decisions. Let them know you, too, are anxious to help them, at any time.

Outside Activities:

Recommend they search the scriptures for examples of struggling by Biblical characters. They should study the way the situation was handled and the resolution of it, later reporting what they learned.

What Do I Do On Sunday?

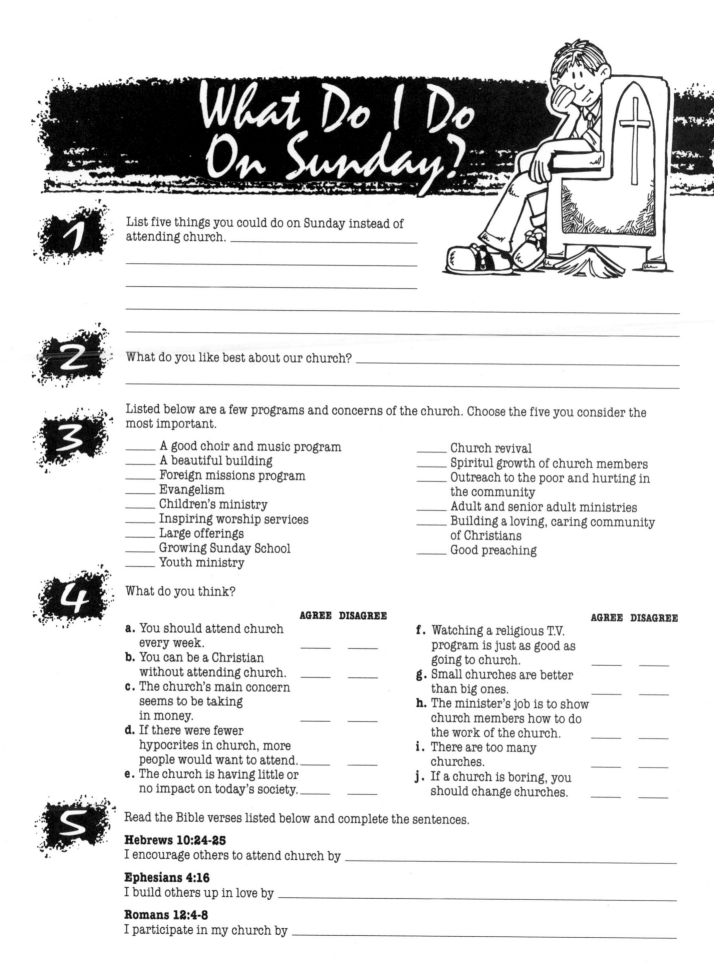

1 List five things you could do on Sunday instead of attending church. _____

_____

_____

_____

_____

2 What do you like best about our church? _____

_____

3 Listed below are a few programs and concerns of the church. Choose the five you consider the most important.

_____ A good choir and music program
_____ A beautiful building
_____ Foreign missions program
_____ Evangelism
_____ Children's ministry
_____ Inspiring worship services
_____ Large offerings
_____ Growing Sunday School
_____ Youth ministry

_____ Church revival
_____ Spiritul growth of church members
_____ Outreach to the poor and hurting in the community
_____ Adult and senior adult ministries
_____ Building a loving, caring community of Christians
_____ Good preaching

4 What do you think?

	AGREE	DISAGREE
a. You should attend church every week.	_____	_____
b. You can be a Christian without attending church.	_____	_____
c. The church's main concern seems to be taking in money.	_____	_____
d. If there were fewer hypocrites in church, more people would want to attend.	_____	_____
e. The church is having little or no impact on today's society.	_____	_____

	AGREE	DISAGREE
f. Watching a religious T.V. program is just as good as going to church.	_____	_____
g. Small churches are better than big ones.	_____	_____
h. The minister's job is to show church members how to do the work of the church.	_____	_____
i. There are too many churches.	_____	_____
j. If a church is boring, you should change churches.	_____	_____

5 Read the Bible verses listed below and complete the sentences.

Hebrews 10:24-25
I encourage others to attend church by _____

Ephesians 4:16
I build others up in love by _____

Romans 12:4-8
I participate in my church by _____

WHAT DO I DO ON SUNDAYS?

Topic: The Church

Purpose of this Session:

This TalkSheet is designed to create discussion about the local church and to encourage young people to be actively involved in it.

To Introduce the Topic:

Ask how many Sundays (total) they have gone to church, in their entire life, so far. Let them try to figure it out an give a prize to the person who comes up with the highest number. Have them estimate how many Sundays they think they will attend church in their lifetime.

You might share your earliest recollection of going to church, or read a few selections from the book *101 THINGS TO DO DURING A DULL SERMON*, by Tim Sims and Dan Pegoda (Youth Specialties), or give them a tour of the sanctuary. Use creative thinking to help them relate to the physical place of "God's House".

The Discussion:

Item #1: Encourage the group to share the different activites that could replace going to church. Talk about the importance or unimportance of each activity in relation to church attendance.

Item #2: Ask the students to enumerate all the things they like about the church. List them on the blackboard. Ask if there is anything they *don't* like and list them as well. Be careful this does not turn into a gripe session.

Item #3: Suggest they pretend they are church board members and to determine priorities for the church's business. Ask which ministries they would discontinue, which they would keep, which they would emphasize.

You might wish to try this hypothetical situation: A rich widow has just died and her will leaves three million dollars to the church. How would they use the money?

Item #4: Have a "vote" on each of the statements, according to their answers. If everyone agreed on a particular one, go on to the next. If there is a wide difference of opinion, have a pro and con discussion.

Item #5: Read each passage and allow them to share their completed sentences with the goup.

To Close the Session:

The following would be useful to emphasize as you close. Your own substitutions can be used, if you wish.

1. The church is "the Body of Christ" and we are all part of it. Christ is no longer physically present inthe world, but his Body, the Church, is. When you become a Christian, you become part of that Body. There is no such thing as a solitary Christian. We grow in community with each other.

2. The purpose of church is not entertainment. In a worship service, we are not the audience — God is. We come to worship Him and to grow closer to Him. That requires expending some effort on our part.

3. Young people are not the "church of tomorrow". They are the church of today. Help them know they are a vitally important part of the church. Encourage them to get involved.

Outside Activities:

1. Distribute a quiz about the church for your students to fill out, asking different members of the congregation for the answers. Sample questions:

a. Name a missionary our church sponsors and the country where he/she serves.
b. What is our pastor's middle name?
c. What is the name of the church's newsletter?
d. Summarize last Sunday's sermon in 25 words or less.
e. What year was our church founded?
f. Which family in our church has been a member the longest?

STRESSED OUT

1 Stress is:

_____ normal and healthy.
_____ to be avoided at all costs.
_____ Other: _____

2 Check any of the following situations that may have produced stress in your life:

_____ Returning home after curfew.
_____ Breaking up with your boyfriend or girlfriend.
_____ Losing your best friend, who moves away.
_____ Studying late at night for an exam.
_____ Lying to your parents and their discovering it.
_____ Flunking a test.
_____ Being told your parents are getting a divorce.
_____ Giving in to peer pressure.
_____ Applying for a job.
_____ Taking your driver's license test.
_____ Getting bad marks on your report card.
_____ Hearing your parents argue and fight.

_____ Being called on by the teacher and not knowing the answer.
_____ Doing something you know is wrong.
_____ Having a pet die.
_____ Being pressured to have sex.
_____ Being pressured to date.
_____ Worrying that your acne is getting worse.
_____ Going out on your first date.
_____ Arguing with your brother or sister.
_____ Being stopped by a traffic policeman.
_____ Having no money.
_____ Moving to another town.
_____ Getting a terrible haircut.
_____ Fighting with your parents.
_____ Other: _____

3 What is good way to get rid of stress? _____
_____
_____

4 Scott received a call slip directing him to see his counselor during fourth period. He knew she wanted to talk to him about his poor grades. He had overheard his mother talking to the counselor about his grades the day before. Scott doesn't want to face the counselor. He wants to ignore the summons and not show up at all.

What would you do if you were Scott? _____
_____
_____

5 Choose one of the following scriptures to rewrite in your own words.

Psalm 55:22 _____

Proverbs 3:5,6 _____

Matthew 6:33.34 _____

Philippians 4:6,7 _____

I Peter 5:7 _____

31

STRESSED OUT

Topic: Stress

Purpose of this Session:

Stress is a fact of life for young people as well as adults. Unfortunately, the youth of today face an undeserved amount of stress. Stresses that normally were not experienced until adulthood are now common during the teen years. This TalkSheet will help your group talk about this stress and how, as Christians, they can best handle it.

To Introduce the Topic:

Have your group list the stresses faced by the youth of today and write the list on the chalkboard. The list should be extensive.

Illustrate the effects of stress by using a balloon. As each kind of streses is mentioned, blow a gust of air into the balloon. As the balloon increases in size, the pressure inside increases as well. If it pops, state that unfortunately some people also "pop" when too many stresses occur. How can we as Christians avoid the pressure of too much stress?

The Discussion:

Item #1: Let the group share their different views. Point out the fact that both answers are true at times; stress *is* normal and healthy (it is an internal warning signal denoting a problem that needs to be dealt with) and there are other times when it should be avoided. Everyone needs a certain amount of stress-free time. Some people need more than others.

Item #2: This exercise brings the topic closer to home. Focus on how they feel when faced with pressures and how they handled each different situation. Be sensitive to their possible embarrassment and don't encourage them to reveal a possible family secret. Try to avoid any additional stress imposed by this activity.

Item #3: Discuss the different ways they can handle stress in their lives. Bring up the negative, destructive things used by some to handle stress (sex, drugs, alcohol, vandalism) and talk about how counterproductive they are, usually only producing more stress. One of the best ways to deal with stress is to talk it over with God in prayer and with a good friend or a counselor.

Item #4: Use this "Tension Getter" to lead into a discussion about the rationalization and avoidance techniques we use to avoid facing stress.

Item #5: Divide the group into smaller ones, having each interpret one of these verses as regards stress. Encourage them to be creative in their interpretations, concentrating on specific teen-age problems.

To Close the Session:

Emphasize the normalcy of some stress in our lives and point out that unresolved stress can wear us down, both physically and mentally. Stress needs to be dealt with.

Help the young people understand they do not have to face stress alone. As Christians, we can "bear each other's burdens" and be a helpful resource for each other. Tell them the church is always there to help; you and the pastor are available and willing to listen and help them deal with their problems. Encourage them to set aside a certain time each day to be with God, an important habit to develop and a healthy way to handle stress.

Outside Activities:

1. Ask that they telephone three other friends in the group during the upcoming week and encourage them.

2. Have them ask their parents how they handle stress as adults and how they handled it as teenagers. They can share their input with the group.

3. Another way to relieve stress is to exercise physically — to "work out" the tension. Organize a "jogging club" for those who would like to run two or three times a week. Another way is to concentrate on someone else's problems, not one's own, making an effort to help. Involve them in a service project in the community.

LOOKING UP

1 Circle the words that best describe a typical worship service at your church:

Terrific	Inspiring	Boring	Mysterious
Exciting	Long	Interesting	Happy
Dramatic	Strange	Formal	Fun
Entertaining	Friendly	Evangelistic	Embarrassing

2 What do you think is the most important part of a worship service? _____
_____
_____

3 Complete this sentence:

If I could change one thing about my church's worship service, it would be _____
_____
_____

4 What do you think? A=AGREE   NS=NOT SURE   D=DISAGREE

	A	NS	D
a. The best place to worship God is in church.	—	—	—
b. I feel close to God when I worship on Sunday morning.	—	—	—
c. Teenagers should have their own worship service.	—	—	—
d. The main purpose of a worship service is to praise God.	—	—	—
e. The time I spend alone with God in prayer, thought and Bible reading is just as important as Sunday morning worship.	—	—	—

	A	NS	D
f. I don't get anything out of sermons.	—	—	—
g. It is not necessary to "dress up" for worship.	—	—	—
h. A good worship service should be entertaining.	—	—	—
i. The songs we sing during the service help me worship God.	—	—	—
j. The service helps me live the Christian life during the week.	—	—	—
k. I would feel good about bringing friends to our worship service.	—	—	—

5 Read one of the following passages of scripture and decide what it says about worshipping God in our church.

John 4:20-24   _____
I Chronicles 16:23-33 _____
2 Kings 21:19-22   _____
Revelation 4:8-11   _____

LOOKING UP

Topic: Worship

Purpose of this Session:

Young people often do not understand the true meaning of worship. Many think of it as a boring meeting that their parents make them attend against their will. This TalkSheet provides you with the opportunity to discuss your church service with them and to encourage them to take it more seriously.

To Introduce the Topic:

Before beginning the discussion using the TalkSheet, conduct a mini-worship service. Have each element of the service in a different room or area in order to distinguish between them. Include a time of fellowship, singing, prayer, scripture reading, teaching and offering.

The Discussion:

Item #1: Ask everyone to explain why they chose the words they did. Do not put down nor argue with those who might choose "boring".

Item #2: It might be helpful to provide copies of your church's bulletin for their reference. Make a list of all the ingredients of a worship service and ask which they think is most important. Discuss the reasons for each different part of the order of worship.

Item #3: Allow a discussion of the parts of the service the young people do not like. Point out that some will be boring, but this does not necessarily make them unacceptable or without purpose. If they have legitimate problems accepting the style of worship, offer to take them to the pastor or to the church's worship committee for further discussion to resolve their discontent.

Item #4: This exercise focuses on the different aspects of worship and the service itself. Let them debate the statements that are controversial. You may wish to express your own opinion, adding that there are indeed many ways to worship God. For instance, we worship God whenever we obey Him and do His will. But that doesn't mean we shouldn't go to church on Sundays. We should worship God whenever we have the opportunity.

Item #5: Ask them to share any insights they might have gained from reading these scriptures.

To Close the Session:

Emphasize the fact that "worship" is a verb. It is something we "do" rather than something that is designed only to inspire or entertain us. They will "get out of it" only as much as they are willing to "put in". Suggest ways for them to participate in the service. This doesn't necessarily mean to participate in the actual program. It means our hearts and minds are focusing on God. Theologian/philosopher Soren Kierkegaard said, "When you leave a worship service, you should not ask 'What did I get out of it?' but 'How did I do?' "

Help them understand we worship God because he loves us unconditionally. In a worship service, we have the opportunity to let Him know we love Him in return. We live in a busy world, which makes it difficult to hear the "still, small voice of God". A worship service gives us a reprieve from the hustle and bustle, and enables us to hear as God speaks to us and to feel nourished when he feeds our spiritual needs. Encourage them to attend worship regularly and to make it a priority in their lives. Close the session by sharing praises to God and prayer requests.

Outside Activities:

1. Plan a worship service, allowing them to be as creative and different as they wish. Have them meet with the pastor and members of the congregation to discuss their ideas.

2. Ask some of your youth to become volunteers for different parts of the morning service, such as scripture reading, ushering, offering, greeting, etc.

THE CHOICE IS YOURS

1 List three BIG decisions (I mean BIG!) you must make for your life in the future. After each, write the date you hope to have decided.

	DECISION	DATE
1.	_____	_____
2.	_____	_____
3.	_____	_____

2 Rank the following decisions from the easiest to make (1) to the most difficult (10).

a. _____ Whether or not to attend youth group meetings.
b. _____ What video or movie to watch.
c. _____ What to do after school.
d. _____ The kind of music to listen to.
e. _____ What to eat for dinner.
f. _____ What clothes to wear to school.

g. _____ When to pray.
h. _____ What to do on Friday and Saturday nights.
i. _____ What kind of friends to have.
j. _____ What to spend money on.
k. _____ Other: _____

3 After each of the following questions, write the letter **A** (Always), **S** (Sometimes) or **N** (Never).

a. Do you have difficulty making up your mind? _____

b. Do you have too many choices in your life? _____

c. Do you consider the consequences of your decisions before making them? _____

d. Do you change your mind after you have made a decision? _____

4 Which of the following things would be most helpful in making a big decision?

a. _____ asking your parent's advice
b. _____ praying about it
c. _____ waiting a few days before deciding
d. _____ reading a horoscope
e. _____ asking a friend
f. _____ looking at the possible consequences of the decision
g. _____ making a decision as quickly as possible

h. _____ flipping a coin
i. _____ doing what everyone else does (going with the crowd)
j. _____ letting someone else decide for you
k. _____ finding scripture that gives direction
l. _____ going with what "feels right"
m. _____ Other: _____

5 What do the following scriptures have to say about making decisions:

Matthew 6:33 _____

_____

Proverbs 3:5-6 _____

_____

1 Peter 5:8 _____

_____

Date Used: _____

Group: _____

THE CHOICE IS YOURS

Topic: Making Decisions

Purpose of this Session:

Young people are faced with making a multitude of decisions, but have very little decision-making experience. They need practice in making good decisions. This TalkSheet will give them an opportunity to learn about making decisions from a Christian point-of-view.

To Introduce the Topic:

Wrap up three gifts to be given to the group. One can be big, another small, one beautifully decorated, another plain, etc. Tell them one of the gifts contains something they would like to receive, one contains something worthless and the other contains nothing at all. Divide them into three groups to decide which gift each group would like to have. They can only look at the gifts, not open them. Once they have made up their minds, draw straws to see which group has the first choice, then the second and the third.

After much disagreement a decision will eventually be reached. Give each group the gift they have chosen. (The good one can contain candy or some inexpensive but desirable prize; the bad ones can contain trash or be empty.) Tell them since they had such a difficult time deciding among themselves, perhaps it would be a good idea to discuss the issue of decision-making.

The Discussion:

Item #1: Ask what "big decisions" they anticipate making in the future and discuss them, identifying those they have in common.

Item #2: Invite them to share their hardest decisions as well as their easiest ones. Ask why some were more difficult than others and encourage their sharing the others they listed.

Item #3: Ask for a show of hands in response to these questions. Focus on "c" because young people don't often think about the consequences of their decisions. In a situation such as whether or not to accept drugs from a friend at a party, ask them to brainstorm all the consequences as well as the benefits. Are the potential consequences worth it? Impulsive decisions that could be harmful can often be checked by remembering to ask yourself, "And then what?"

Item #4: Discuss the practical how-to's of making decisions: (1) gather all the facts, (2) consider all the alternatives, (3) get some good advice, (4) pray and (5) choose the best alternative.

Item #5: Lead them into relating these scriptures to practical situations. Encourage them to seek God's perspective when making decisions.

To Close the Session:

It is important they understand the big decisions they are making are nothing more than a combination of all the little decisions they have made. The choices they make today are building the foundation for the rest of their lives. If they can develop the habit of making wise decisions about the little things, they will be much more secure and confident when they are faced with the bigger ones to come.

Explain that the ability to make decisions is an indication of maturity. Some people don't know how to make commitments to anything; they get "stuck" and never grow up. Sometimes they wait for someone else to take the responsibility of a decision. Ask them to think about what kind of person they want to be, what kind of life they want to live.

Emphasize that making a wrong decision once in a while is certainly human and permissable. They should be cautioned against letting the fear of making a wrong decision freeze them into deciding nothing. As Christians, we can be confident about making decisions, not because they will always be correct, but because they will be forgiven, if wrong.

Outside Activites:

1. Ask them to write down, on a 3x5 card, a problem or situation that needs a decision. These need not be identified with their names. Re-distribute the cards to the group so each person has another's problem. During the following week, they can study the problem and bring their solution to the next session. If they know whose card they have, they can discuss the problem with that person, pray about it with them and try to help them reach a wise decision.

2. Have your group develop a presentation for your junior high group entitled, "Decisions Christians must make in high school."

DOING · DRUGS

1 List two or three reasons why you think high school students use drugs.

_____

_____

_____

2 In your high school, how many students do you think use drugs on a regular basis? (Circle one.)

0%   10%   20%   30%   40%   50%   60%   70%   80%   90%   100%

3 If you could talk to a third grade class about drug abuse, what would you tell them? List three main points from your talk on the back of this sheet.

4 What do you think?

	AGREE	DISAGREE			AGREE	DISAGREE
a. The dangers of experimenting with drugs far outweigh the benefits of trying them.	___	___	**d.** Occasional drug use will not be harmful to a young person.		___	___
b. Drugs can have a positive influence on a person's life.	___	___	**e.** Drinking alcohol is just as bad as taking drugs.		___	___
c. If a friend were to offer me drugs, he/she should look elsewhere for friends.	___	___	**f.** Parents should talk regularly with their children about drug abuse.		___	___

5 Every guy in the locker room had a story about "getting wasted" after Friday's game. Last Monday they were swapping sex stories. Today the topic is how Jeff got loaded, how Todd won the beer chugging contest at Wendy's party and how Bill smoked the best weed ever. Mark asked Steve if he also got wasted Friday night; Steve had gone to his church's youth group party.

What are Steve's choices? _____

_____

What should Steve do? _____

_____

6 Read the following scripture verses and write out how you think each verse relates to substance abuse.

I Corinthians 3:16-17 _____

I Corinthians 10:31 _____

Romans 12:1-2 _____

I Corinthians 10:13 _____

Galatians 6:7 _____

DOING DRUGS

Topic: Drugs and Substance Abuse

Purpose of this Session:

America is a drugged society. Drugs are everywhere, from medicine cabinet sleeping pills to cocaine in the executive washroom. Young people are under terrible pressure to experiment with drugs. This TalkSheet will give you a chance to discuss a Christian response to the drug problem.

To Introduce the Session:

Interview four to six people about drug abuse in advance of this discussion. Tape the interviews and play them for the group. Try to obtain several differing opinions.

Read aloud an article about drug abuse from a magazine or newspaper. Something occurring locally would have more impact. You might also focus on an article that deals with a famous film star or sports hero who has admitted a drug dependency and has undergone rehabilitation and treatment.

The Discussion:

Item #1: Write down all the reasons the group listed. Choose three or four of the most common to discuss. Anticipate their remarking "peer pressure — everybody does it", "getting high — it feels good", and "getting wasted — to escape reality".

Item #2: Expect a wide range of answers on this, even from those who attend the same school. This is not an attempt to discover who is using drugs, so do not permit names to be mentioned. The object is to find out to what extent drugs are being used by those in your area high schools. Follow up with a question such as, "Would you say that drugs are easy to get on your campus, or not?"

Item #3: Ask that they share the comments they would make to the third graders. Find out how many had similar points to make. If your group is outgoing enough, have two or three give a talk as if they were actually speaking to third graders.

Item #4: Open these statements to debate, especially if a difference in opinions exists. Ask for a show of hands regarding the last statement. Ask how many have talked to their parents about drug abuse. It is doubtful there will be many. Encourage them to talk to their parents about drugs. Role-play different parent-teen situations to make conversations with their parents easier.

Item #5: Use this "Tension Getter" to talk about peer pressure to use drugs. Ask them to describe situations in which they have been under pressure to try drugs. Role-play creative ways to say "No".

Item #6: Explain that the Bible does not say, specifically, "Thou shalt not do drugs." Scripture, however, does give us guidelines and principles for making decisions about things that are harmful, like drugs. Read these passages and let several of the students interpret them in relation to drug abuse.

To Close the Session:

In today's world, having fun is often associated with drug use and drinking alcohol. "Partying" is synonymous with "getting wasted" or getting drunk. Ask how many ways the group can think of to have healthy fun instead.

Outside Activities:

1. Have the students compile a dictionary of terms associated with the drug culture. Discuss with them why there is so much drug terminology and how this influences the young people of today.

2. Suggest they compose a "position paper" — a manifesto — which states their official position on drugs and other mind-altering substances. ("Whereas. . . . . , Therefore be it resolved that we, the youth of First Church. . .") Ask all the young people to sign it, embellish it with a large gold seal and post it in a conspicuous place.

KIDS JUST WANT TO HAVE FUN

1 "Fun" equals = _____.
_____

2 I could have more fun, if I changed places with

_____
Name of Person

3 What do you think? A=AGREE, NS=NOT SURE, D=DISAGREE

		A	NS	D			A	NS	D
a.	It is fun being a Christian.	___	___	___	**f.**	I would rather have fun with a few friends than with a large crowd.	___	___	___
b.	My life is boring.	___	___	___	**g.**	Non-Christian kids don't really have fun; they just think they do.	___	___	___
c.	Christians have a different kind of fun than non-Christians.	___	___	___	**h.**	Most fun things are either sinful or unhealthy.	___	___	___
d.	I need more excitement and fun than the average teenager.	___	___	___					
e.	When I am having fun, I sometimes don't care what might happen to me.	___	___	___					

4 Rank the activities below from the most fun (1) to the least fun (10).

_____ Hobbies   _____ Daydreaming   _____ Work
_____ Partying   _____ Watching television _____ Being with friends
_____ Family vacations _____ Playing sports   _____ Youth group
_____ Dating   _____ School

5 Read the following scripture verses and write out what you think each has to say about having fun.

Deuteronomy 12:7 _____

_____

Ecclesiastes 2:24-25 _____

_____

John 10:10 _____

_____

Mark 8:36 _____

_____

Ephesians 5:15-16 _____

_____

Date Used: _____

Group: _____

KIDS JUST WANT TO HAVE FUN

Topic: Fun

Purpose of this Session:

Many young people do not know how to have fun. Teenagers are trying to act like adults at such an early age they haven't had time to learn how to play. If a person acts silly or crazy (healthily uninhibited) young people are either embarrassed or think the person is stoned or drunk. Having fun creatively and safely is important to learn. This TalkSheet will help you explore the facets of having fun.

To Introduce the Topic:

Offer a prize to a volunteer who thinks they can last one minute without smiling or laughing. Challenge the rest to try and make the volunteer laugh, giggle or crack a smile. Anything is permitted, except touching. Let others try remaining "stone-faced" in turn.

Use an ice breaker or a game from the Youth Specialties *Ideas* library or the book *Play It* (Youth Specialties/Zondervan). Choose a simple game that can be completed quickly and will generate laughter.

The Discussion:

Item #1: Make a master list of all their definitions of "fun". There may be both positive and negative answers. Keep the list in view in case you wish to refer to it.

Item #2: Ask the students to explain why they chose the person they named.

Item #3: Read the statements aloud and ask for volunteers to express their opinion. Some require more self-revelation than others, so be sensitive to their feelings. Some may require further discussion. Ask that they explain their answers. For example, some might disagree to the statement "It is fun being a Christian."

Some of the statements explore the need of some for constant excitement. Young people who are always "living on the edge" are headed for trouble. Partying has become a major sport. Fun is healthy and good but destructive "fun" can be potentially dangerous.

Ask the members of your group why they think so many young people choose to have fun in harmful ways, such as substance abuse.

Item #4: Ask them to share their choices for "most fun" and "least fun". Discuss healthy, safe ways to have fun.

Item #5: Read the scriptures and ask the group what the Bible has to say about having fun. Try dividing the students into smaller groups for this part of the discussion.

To Close the Session:

Try to make these key points:

(1) God does want us to have fun. He is not a "cosmic killjoy" sitting up in Heaven with a frown on his face. He wants us to enjoy life at its fullest. He is the Creator of life and therefore, He knows what is best for us and how we might get the most out of life. Read Phillipians 4:4. Paul encourages us to "rejoice!"

(2) Challenge your students to consider partying without drugs or alcohol. Getting wasted is not only *not* fun, but it can also invite serious criminal charges as well as lead to permanent brain damage. Encourage them to group date without pairing off. Going out with a group of friends is a great way to have fun and to get to know each other better.

Outside Activities:

Plan a party at the home of one of the group members. *Creative Socials and Special Events* by Wayne Rice and Mike Yaconelli is a good resource book (Youth Specialties/Zondervan).

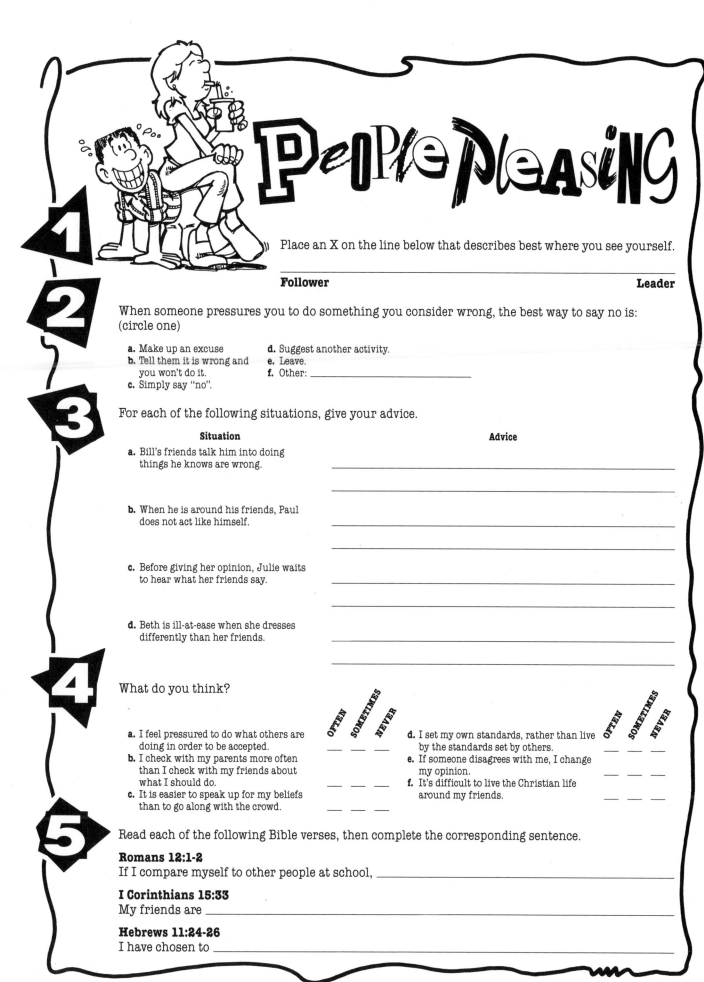

PEOPLE PLEASING

1 Place an X on the line below that describes best where you see yourself.

_____

Follower   **Leader**

2 When someone pressures you to do something you consider wrong, the best way to say no is: (circle one)

a. Make up an excuse   **d.** Suggest another activity.
b. Tell them it is wrong and   **e.** Leave.
    you won't do it.   **f.** Other: _____
c. Simply say "no".

3 For each of the following situations, give your advice.

Situation	Advice
a. Bill's friends talk him into doing things he knows are wrong.	_____ _____
b. When he is around his friends, Paul does not act like himself.	_____ _____
c. Before giving her opinion, Julie waits to hear what her friends say.	_____ _____
d. Beth is ill-at-ease when she dresses differently than her friends.	_____ _____

4 What do you think?

OFTEN   SOMETIMES   NEVER

a. I feel pressured to do what others are doing in order to be accepted. — — —
b. I check with my parents more often than I check with my friends about what I should do. — — —
c. It is easier to speak up for my beliefs than to go along with the crowd. — — —

OFTEN   SOMETIMES   NEVER

d. I set my own standards, rather than live by the standards set by others. — — —
e. If someone disagrees with me, I change my opinion. — — —
f. It's difficult to live the Christian life around my friends. — — —

5 Read each of the following Bible verses, then complete the corresponding sentence.

Romans 12:1-2
If I compare myself to other people at school, _____

I Corinthians 15:33
My friends are _____

Hebrews 11:24-26
I have chosen to _____

PEOPLE PLEASING

Topic: Peer Pressure

Purpose of this Session:

The pressures on young people to conform to a behavior pattern dictated by their peers is increasing. They are trying to emulate their ideas of adulthood at younger and younger ages and are spending less and less time interacting with responsible adults. They attend classes with their peers, work at jobs employing a lot of people their age and, when at home, confer with their friends by telephone. This TalkSheet explores ways for Christian young people to resist misguided peer pressure.

To Introduce the Topic:

Announce to the group you are going to have a "taste test" in which they will be asked to determine which of two brands of punch they like the best, brand A or brand B. Give each person a small paper cup of punch from each unmarked pitcher.

Prior to the test, ask a few "influential" persons to deliberately choose brand A as the best. They will try to persuade the others to choose the same one. Chances are good the others will yield to this "peer pressure", even though *both brands are exactly the same*.

If others stick to their own convictions, congratulate them for having successfully resisted peer pressure. They may have some insights to share.

The Discussion:

Item #1: Discuss the difference in being a leader and in being a follower. Ask the students to brainstorm the characteristics of each. Point out there is nothing wrong with being a follower (without followers there would be no leaders), but the trick is to make certain those you are following know where they are going. Many make the mistake of following the crowd to attain a sense of belonging. Unfortunately, the crowd doesn't always know right from wrong. Many followers can set an example for others, thereby becoming leaders themselves.

Item #2: Ask the students to share their responses and discuss other alternatives to negative peer pressure.

Item #3: These true-to-life situations will provide practical experience in dealing with similar ones in their own lives. Let them share advice and creative responses with each other.

Item #4: Discuss these statements in a general way, being careful not to embarrass anyone. Each deals with a specific aspect of peer pressure and will help students evaluate their own vulnerability. Choose one or two to emphasize, such as the one regarding parents. Ask them how they can decide what to do if they do not talk to their parents when their friends are pressuring them. Try to help them stretch their minds and think through the consequences of giving in. Guide them into understanding the results of their actions.

Item #5: Allow students to share their completed sentences. A pertinent Bible verse to discuss and memorize is I Corinthians 15:33.

To Close the Session:

Encourage the group to realize they can avoid situations which might cause them to succumb to unacceptable peer pressure. If their friends constantly pressure them to do things they feel are wrong, they need to find new friends. True friends do not try to force others to do things they don't believe in.

The philosopher Soren Kierkegaard wrote, "There is a view of life which says that where the crowd is, there is also the truth. There is another view of life which conceives that wherever there is a crowd, there is untruth." Regardless of which view is correct, it is important the students understand the advantage of being a bit *skeptical* of what the crowd does. There is a strong possibility the values of the world are going to be in opposition to the values of the kingdom of God. We need to "seek first the kingdom of God" (Matthew, 6:33) to help us consistently make the right decision.

Discuss the fact that Christ also was tempted in all things, just as we are, and He understands. Christ can help in our struggle and the power of the Holy Spirit will enable us to have "self-control" — a fruit of the spirit — rather than be crowd-controlled. Asking for God's help through daily prayer is essential for mental strength and health.

Outside Activities:

1. Assign an interview with parents, asking what peer pressures the parents experienced as young people and as adults.

2. Suggest a "scripture search" to find examples of peer pressure and how it was handled, such as Matthew 4:1-11 and 26:69-75. Discuss the research.

Honestly

1 Rank the following from the most dishonest (1) to the least dishonest (6).

a. _____ Lying to parents in order to get permission to go out.

b. _____ Cheating on a test.

c. _____ Shoplifting.

d. _____ Giving a falsified excuse to the teacher.

e. _____ Protecting a friend by lying.

f. _____ Goofing off when you are being paid to work.

2 What do you think? Beside each statement, write Yes or No.

a. _____ A student can get through school without lying.

b. _____ The truth should always be told, no matter what the consequences are.

c. _____ If we want to make it to the top in life, we will have to be a little dishonest at times.

d. _____ People cannot be true friends if they are not honest with each other.

e. _____ There are times when it is impossible to be honest with parents.

f. _____ Lying can sometimes be an act of kindness.

g. _____ Lying is permissable as long as it doesn't hurt anyone and we don't get caught.

h. _____ It is acceptable to tell an occasional "white lie".

3 Imagine yourself in the following situations:

a. A friend is telling other people lies about someone you know in the cafeteria during lunch. **What would you do?**

_____ Say nothing.   _____ Change the subject.   _____ Confront the person about the lies.

b. In the locker room, you find a math book with someone's name written in pencil on the inside cover. **What would you do?**

_____ Try to sell it back to the bookstore after erasing the name.

_____ Leave the book in the locker room.

_____ Turn the book in to the office so the rightful owner can be notified.

c. A good friend has a new haircut that is very unflattering, but the friend seems to like it. Your friend asks your opinion. **What would you do?**

_____ Say it looks great.

_____ Avoid giving an answer.

_____ Risk hurting your friend's feelings by trying to be tactful and telling the truth.

4 What do you think is meant by the phrase "Honesty is the Best Policy"? _____

_____

5 On the back of this sheet, summarize **Psalm 15:1-3** in twenty words or less.

Date Used: _____

Group: _____

HONESTLY

Topic: Honesty

Purpose of this Session:

Honesty is an important topic to discuss with young people because dishonesty is all around them. Lying to parents, cheating on exams and dishonesty at work are all considered accepted behavior in today's culture. This TalkSheet is designed to facilitate a discussion on the key issues regarding honesty and the Christian.

To Introduce the Topic:

Ask your group members to sit in a circle, or circles, if you have a large group. With the room darkened, have one person shine a flashlight (the spotlight) on another's face and ask them a question, to be answered as honestly as possible. Only the person in the "spotlight" may speak. This will focus everyone's attention on the one sharing. The questions can be as deep or as shallow as you wish, and no one is required to answer if they are uncomfortable. To begin with, ask questions such as "What is your middle name?", "Who was the first person of the opposite sex you liked?" and "What were you doing on the night of _____?" Do not pass judgment on what is shared. After several have shared, turn the lights back on and announce you will be discussing honesty.

Playing the game "Whopper" is another way to begin. On a piece of paper, the students write down three statements about themselves, only one of which is true. In turn, the group tries to guess which is the true statement. Young people are so clever few will be able to guess the correct one.

The Discussion:

Item #1: Ask that they reveal their choices and give reasons. Expect considerable disagreement and encourage debating about the different answers.

Item #2: There may be some difficulty with this exercise because the answers must be either yes or no. Divide them according to their answers and allow them to debate the issues. You may want to focus on the hot issue, "There are times when it is impossible to be honest with parents."

Another important statement is, "Lying is okay. . .if you don't get caught." Even though most won't admit it, many of them believe this. Help them see the fallacy of this kind of reasoning.

The last one, concerning "white lies", is also worthy of extra time. Ask them to give examples of what they consider "white" or "black" lies. Remind them lies are still lies and it is never safe to assume some are permissable while others are not.

Item #3: These "Tension Getters" offer some true-to-life situations to bring up for discussion. Allow them to share what they would actually do. Keep the general attitude open and free from put-downs or they will be inclined to "lie" about their answers and merely tell you what they think you want to hear.

Item #4: Discuss what God has to say about honesty. One of the ten commandments is directly concerned with honesty. God knows what is best for us. Honesty pays off in the long run. There may be rare exceptions to this rule, such as the experience of Corrie Ten Boom, who lied to Nazi soldiers in order to save the lives of the Jews who were hiding in her home, but we can trust God to bless us for being honest. Challenge the students to try to imagine how God would think on this question.

Item #5: Ask them to read their paraphrases. In addition to Psalm 15:1-3, you may ask them to read the scriptures and find a few proverbs relating to honesty.

To Close the Session:

Summarize what has been discussed. Focus some of your concluding remarks on the consequences of honesty and dishonesty. Help them see lying only breeds more lies and eventually the situation disintegrates. One of the true characteristics of a Christian is honesty and trustworthiness. Reinforce God's forgiveness for past dishonesty.

Outside Activities:

1. Ask the students to interview their parents about their feelings of honesty, including some questions about their own parent-child relationship. Honesty in family life is often a difficult achievement. Encourage parent-teen interaction on the subject.

2. Ask them to search for examples of dishonesty in newspapers and magazines. They will be amazed at how much there is in advertising, in politics and in business. Share these examples at the beginning of the next session.

We Are The World

1   If you could do one thing to make the world a better place, **what would you do?** _____
_____
_____

2   Which of the following should Christians be most concerned about? Choose five, ranking them from 1 (most concerned) to 5 (least concerned).

a. _____ Problems in Central America
b. _____ Poverty
c. _____ Violence on television
d. _____ Racism
e. _____ Sexual exploitation of women and children
f. _____ Pornography
g. _____ Crime
h. _____ Hunger
i. _____ Terrorism
j. _____ Threat of nuclear war
k. _____ Prayer in the schools
l. _____ Homosexuality
m. _____ Materialism
n. _____ Abortion
o. _____ Over population
p. _____ Divorce
q. _____ AIDS
r. _____ Child abuse
s. _____ Other: _____
_____

3   What do you think?

a. One person cannot make a significant difference in today's society. ☐ **FOR SURE** ☐ **NO WAY**

b. The world's problems will eventually be solved by science and technology.
☐ **FOR SURE**   ☐ **NO WAY**

c. The world hunger situation is God's will and we should not try to change it.   ☐ **FOR SURE** ☐ **NO WAY**

d. The church can solve the problems of the world. ☐ **FOR SURE**   ☐ **NO WAY**

e. The welfare system will eventually solve the problems of the poor. ☐ **FOR SURE** ☐ **NO WAY**

f. The poor are responsible for their situation.
☐ **FOR SURE**   ☐ **NO WAY**

g. The world's problems should not concern Christians because Christ is returning soon.
☐ **FOR SURE**   ☐ **NO WAY**

4   Put an **X** on the line below indicating how much you think you are involved in making a difference in the world.

None at all _____ **A lot**

Now put an **O** on the line, indicating how much you would *like* to be involved in making a difference in the world.

5   Summarize **Matthew 25:31-46** in twenty words or less. _____
_____
_____

Date Used: _____

Group: _____

WE ARE THE WORLD

Topic: Christian Social Action

Purpose of this Session:

This present generation of young people has been overwhelmed by the problems of the world but, as yet, nothing has inspired them to take positive action. Use this TalkSheet to discuss the Christian responsibility to minister to the needs of others.

To Introduce the Session:

Ask several of the students to volunteer for an experiment. Tie the volunteers' hands and feet securely so they cannot get loose, then give them tasks to do that they obviously can't accomplish while tied up. Push them around, without hurting them. This is to illustrate how it feels to be powerless to do anything for oneself about a given situation. Only after someone else unties them can they do things for themselves. Ask how it felt to be powerless, to be pushed around and exploited and if anyone has the right to keep others tied up, etc.

Suggest the students look through news magazines, such as *TIME* or *NEWSWEEK*, or newspapers to find as many reports as possible about the homeless, the needy and other world problems. Allow five minutes for their search, dividing them into groups and competing for the largest total of news items. Afterward, discuss their findings.

The Discussion:

Item #1: Some may have difficulty answering this question. They may feel overwhelmed by the problems of today and feel like there is nothing they can do. Encourage them to fantasize a little bit. They need to understand *they* can effect change in today's world.

Item #2: This activity forces the students to rank problems according to priority. Let them express their opinions of their concept of the most important problems in the world today. Compare what each has listed and try to compose a master list of ten. Follow up by asking what they think the church can do about any of the problems.

Item #3: Each of these questions has the potential for further discussion. If there is disagreement on any, stop and discuss it. "No way" would be a good answer for each, the point being that God does want His people to be involved in helping others. We may not be able to solve all the world's problems, but God can use us to touch others' lives. The last thing we should be doing when Jesus returns is to be sitting around on our hands. Remember, young people need to know they can make a difference in spite of the overwhelming immensity of our world's problems.

Item #4: This exercise illustrates the difference between what they are doing now and what they would like to be doing. Ask for suggestions about how they would actually go about making the world a better place. List the ideas.

Item #5: Ask them to read their summaries and describe one thing they learned from this passage.

To Close the Session:

Bring out the fact that God wants to use each person in the room to make a difference in the world. Remind them of the "Feeding of the Five Thousand" in scripture. Jesus was able to take a small boy's sack lunch and feed a multitude with it. In the same way, God can take whatever we have to offer, no matter how small and insignificant, and bless it. In God's economy, "little is much when God is in it."

Outside Activities:

A mission or service project would obviously be appropriate. An excellent resource for ideas on planning and projects is the book *Ideas for Social Action* by Anthony Campolo (Youth Specialties/Zondervan). Involve the students in the planning in order for them to have a sense of "ownership".

ONE IS A LONELY NUMBER

1 List five words that describe loneliness.

a. _____

b. _____   d. _____

c. _____   e. _____

2 Complete the following sentence: The worst kind of loneliness would be _____
_____

3 It's a boring Saturday afternoon. Buffy is at the mall with three of her friends. She likes them, but she doesn't think she fits in. That night in her diary, she writes about how lonely she feels. **Why do you think Buffy feels lonely?** _____
_____

4 What do you think? A=AGREE   NS=NOT SURE   D=DISAGREE

	A	NS	D
a. Everyone is lonely at some time.	___	___	___
b. If someone is with people, he/she will not be lonely.	___	___	___
c. If a person feels lonely, it is his/her own fault.	___	___	___
d. If life were more exciting, young people would not be lonely.	___	___	___
e. Jesus Christ felt lonely.	___	___	___
f. If you feel lonely when you are young, you will be lonely for the rest of your life.	___	___	___

5 When a person is lonely, he/she should . . . (Mark your choice of solutions and add your own ideas.)

___ Find new friends.
___ Spend time in prayer with God.
___ Feel sorry for yourself.
___ Look for new and different things to do.
___ Become irritable and take your feelings out on others.

___ Worry.
___ Learn to be a better friend.
___ Feel hopeless and helpless.
___ Stop putting yourself down.

___ Go for a walk.
___ Don't compare yourself to others.
___ Enjoy being alone as a sign of maturity.
___ Read a Psalm.
___ Help someone else.

6 Read **II Timothy 4:16-18**

What do you think Paul felt? _____
_____

Why do other people not always support us? _____
_____

How do you think the Lord supported Paul? _____
_____

Date Used: _____

Group: _____

ONE IS A LONELY NUMBER

Topic: Loneliness

Purpose of this Session:

Adults often say the teen years are the best years of a young person's life. Adults forget teenagers can be very lonely in the midst of all the fun. This TalkSheet offers your group the opportunity to air their feelings of loneliness, the causes and cures, and how God can help.

To Introduce the Topic:

Tell your group you are all going to make up a story about loneliness. Begin by saying "Skip was getting ready for school when. . .", then a student adds the next part of the plot. Let volunteers keep the story going, the only rules being it should be kept clean and be about loneliness. You are sure to end up with a good introduction to a discussion on "loneliness".

The Discussion:

Item #1: Make a master list of all the words chosen and keep it visually accessible for later referral, if needed.

Item #2: Ask the students to share what they believe would be the worst kinds of loneliness. Talk about their choices.

Item #3: This "Tension Getter" will invite discussion about the difference between "loneliness" and "being alone". Loneliness is usually a feeling inside oneself, perhaps of being misunderstood, or unappreciated. There may be feelings of inferiority causing one to feel lonely, even when surrounded by people. These underlying emotions need to be considered. The difference between loneliness and boredom is also important to bring out at this time. Some young people feel lonely because they are bored, which is normal and can be remedied easily.

Item #4: Discuss each of these statements with your group. Allow them to express their thoughts on each one. Take the time needed to allow for any disagreements. Tell them Christ also felt lonely (Matthew 13:53-57, Luke 4:24-30, Mark 14:22,27,31,50, Mark 15:1-34). Loneliness is not necessarily a bad state of mind. In today's world, young people feel a great need to be entertained all the time. Sometimes they need to learn it's all right to be alone and lonely once in a while.

The last statement is designed to help them realize loneliness is not a terminal disease. It has a cure. We should not let ourselves become overwhelmed by it.

Item #5: Some practical and concrete solutions to loneliness can be evaluated here.

Item #6: Describe how Paul faced his loneliness. Ask your group if God can do the same for them as He did for Paul. You might also wish to read Psalm 146.

To Close the Session:

Emphasize God created us to have mutually affirming relationships with other people and that's one reason we feel lonely at times. We are social creatures and need to live in families and in community with others. We cease to function well when totally alone. That's another reason God created the church, which is a group of people called together by God to love and care for each other. Try a community-building activity, such as one of the hundreds found in the *Ideas* series published by Youth Specialties. *Building Community in Youth Groups* by Denny Rydberg (Group Books) is another good resource.

Outside Activities:

1. Ask the group to search the scriptures for examples of loneliness and to find out how the Biblical characters resolved their situation, sharing their findings at the next meeting.

2. Suggest creative skits with the theme "loneliness". Groups of two or three can then act out their skits for the others. Humor is permissable but the skits should include some method of resolution.

WISE UP

1 Who is the wisest person you know?

_____

2 What is the best advice anyone ever gave you?

_____

3 Complete this sentence:
I would be much wiser if I _____

_____

_____

_____

4 Areas in which I need more wisdom are: (check all that are appropriate)

_____ school work   _____ choosing friends
_____ family life   _____ use of money
_____ controlling emotions _____ listening to advice
_____ my sex life   _____ my future
_____ understanding the Bible _____ others: _____

5 What advice would you give to the mother who wrote this letter?

> _Dear Senior High Student,_
>   _I am the mother of three — two teenaged daughters and one teenaged son. My problem is that none of them will listen to my advice. They think they know it all and that I know nothing, especially my son, the oldest. I'm concerned for their future and want to share some of my hard-earned wisdom. I don't want them to make the same mistakes I made or those I have seen others make. What do I do?_
>
>   _A Mother at the End of A Rope._

_____

_____

_____

_____

_____

6 Read a chapter in the Book of Proverbs. Then write five pieces of advice given in the chapter.

1. _____

2. _____

3. _____

4. _____

5. _____

Date Used: _____

Group: _____

WISE UP

Topic: Wisdom

Purpose of this Session:

The youth of today get advice from all sides: friends, teachers, parents, the media. To whom will they listen the most? This TalkSheet was designed to discuss the need for wisdom in guiding one's life and the need for God's Word to be the ultimate source of that wisdom.

To Introduce this Session:

Ask several of the students to share with the group one of the "dumbest things" they have ever done. Most will have plenty of experiences to choose from. Make a humorous game out of it and have them write their situations anonymously on cards. Then, as you read each one, ask the rest of the group to try and guess who wrote it.

Introduce the TalkSheet by saying "Everybody does something dumb once in a while, but hopefully, we learn from these experiences and get a little wiser. That's what we're going to talk about now: wisdom and how to get it."

The Discussion:

Item #1: Ask the members of the group to share the names of the people they consider wise. Ask why they chose them.

Item #2: Ask for volunteers to share their bits of good advice.

Item #3: Let some of the students read their completed sentences and state their reasons. Close by making the point that all of us seek more wisdom, each day of our lives.

Item #4: After listening to their answers, point out being "wise" doesn't necessarily mean being "smart". As the old saying goes, "Scholars are a dime a dozen, but a man of wisdom is rare indeed." Learning is one thing; what you do with your learning is wisdom. We should use wisdom in every area of daily living.

Item #5: This letter deals with a problem common to parents of teenagers — the know-it-all son or daughter. As the students share their advice to the mother, try to help them see the parent's point of view, rather than just their own.

Item #6: This exercise is appropriate for several small groups. Make certain each takes a different chapter. Allow sufficient time for them to think of five statements of wise advice. The purpose is learning to use the Bible as a source of wisdom for daily living. Encourage them to look at God's Word for help in practical ways.

To Close the Session:

Talk about the importance of seeking God's wisdom through prayer, Bible study and the counsel of other Christians. Challenge them to be skeptical of and to carefully evaluate the advice they hear from their friends, the media, etc. Remind them of the wisest proverb of all: "The fear of God is the beginning of wisdom." (Prov. 1:7) True wisdom comes from God; the more we love God and keep His commandments, the more wisdom we receive.

Outside Activities:

1. Together, choose five topics everyone would most like advice on, such as choosing friends, dealing with anger or resisting drugs. Ask them to find out what the Bible says about each one and to report their findings to the group. A good resource is the book *Good Advice* by Todd Temple and Jim Hancock (Youth Specialties, 1987).

2. Divide the meeting into smaller groups, having each choose one of the "wise thoughts" they discovered from the book of Proverbs in Item #6. Have them create and display posters communicating the truth.

LET'S GET PHYSICAL

1 Complete this sentence:
If I could change one thing about my appearance, it

would be _____

2 The money I spend on clothes and appearance is:
(circle one)

not enough   about right
probably too much   ridiculous

3 Rank the following reasons for your choice of fashion style from the best (1) to the worst (8):

_____ I feel comfortable this way.　　　　　_____ I want to please God.
_____ It is what others expect.　　　　　　 _____ My parents approve of this style.
_____ I don't want to be obviously different.　_____ It shows off my body.
_____ I want others to notice me.　　　　　 _____ I want to make a good impression.

4 What do you think?   T=TRUE   F=FALSE

a. If it looks good on, wear it.   T   F
b. I am judged by how attractive I am.   T   F
c. I usually feel self-conscious about
my appearance.   T   F
d. I dress deliberately to attract
attention.   T   F
e. It's acceptable to follow the latest
fads in fashion.   T   F

f. Most people are hung up on
appearance.   T   F
g. Another's appearance doesn't
affect my opinion of them.   T   F
h. People who are good looking have
a big advantage.   T   F

5 Rate the following six categories as to whether or not each

(1) matters very much to God
(2) matters very little to God
(3) matters to God if it matters to me
(4) doesn't matter at all to God.

_____ The way I dress.　　_____ My grooming.　　_____ How physically attractive I am.
_____ My hairstyle.　　　 _____ My weight.　　　_____ How sexy I look.

6 Choose one of the following scriptures to rewrite in your own words.

Proverbs 31:30　　　**1 Samuel 16:7**　　　**1 Timothy 4:7-8**　　　**Psalm 147: 10-11**

_____

_____

_____

_____

_____

_____

_____

_____

_____

LET'S GET PHYSICAL

Topic: Physical appearance

Purpose of this Session:

Personal appearance is important for self-esteem, especially to young people. This TalkSheet gives your group the opportunity to study the subject of physical attractiveness and how it affects them as Christians.

To Introduce the Topic:

Before the meeting, dress yourself differently from your usual attire; change your hairstyle, if possible, or wear a hat. Your outward appearance makes a statement about what kind of person you are. Ask the group what they think your new look says about you.

If you have the use of an overhead projector, draw the outline of a "regular guy" on one transparency and place a blank one on top. Ask for suggested additions to the drawing to make your character look "cool". Sketch a different hairstyle or articles of clothing on the transparency until the desired result is reached. As you distribute this TalkSheet, lift the second transparency pointing out the fact that the person underneath is still the same, no matter how he looks on the outside.

The Discussion:

Item #1: All of us are unhappy with certain areas of our physical selves. To teenagers, these flaws are unrealistically magnified and painful for them to discuss. Remind them of a few ground rules, such as "no put-downs" and "The Golden Rule". Not everyone will want to reveal his or her answer to this question, but if the students are comfortable with each other, a few might. Begin by answering it yourself and describing your feelings as a teenager.

Item #2: Ask the group to "guesstimate" how much average teenagers in several types of subcultures spend on clothing and appearance. For example, if the teen subculture in your community is western, ask the students how much they think the average cowboy spends.

Item #3: This is designed to force the students to think about why they dress and look the way they do. Most state they do not want to conform, yet their appearance reflects the opposite.

Item #4: Since personal appearance can be difficult to discuss, talk about these statements in a general way. Don't ask the students for personal examples; let them volunteer their comments. Don't be fearful of dealing with their hurt, anger and frustration. Assure them these feelings are normal. Stress God's love and acceptance.

The statement "People who are good looking have a big advantage" is deserving of extra discussion. Most will answer "True" and they are probably correct. This is the world's way of judging, but not God's way. Even if we are not good looking, we have a big advantage if we trust God with our lives. Having good looks does not assure happiness and success, which only God can provide.

Item #5: This statement will encourage discussing to what extent God cares about their appearance. Again, do not use their own personal examples, but illustrate with an hypothetical teenager.

Item #6: Give each of several small groups one of the four passages to paraphrase, sharing the results.

To Close the Session:

Summarize the points discovered by the group during the discussion, such as: God cares about our hearts more than our looks and it's permissable to try to look our best — God wants us to look good on the outside as well as on the inside — but we shouldn't be preoccupied with outer appearances. Stress the fact that Christians differ from non-Christians in that we accept and love each other no matter how we look. It would be appropriate to suggest a community-building exercise in which the students affirm each other.

Outside Activities:

1. Ask the group to bring examples from magazine ads of preoccupation with physical appearance. Lead a discussion concerning the reason advertising places emphasis on the physical appearance of models rather than on the product being marketed.

2. Suggest the students notice whether or not there is someone in their school who is being ostracized because of his or her physical appearance. If so, ask that they make a sincere effort to be friendly and accepting to this person by joining them for lunch or inviting them to youth group or some other activity.

Material World

1 Make a wish list of "things" you would like to buy right now. (Use the back of the sheet, if necessary.) _____

_____

_____

_____

2 Write **Y** (Yes) or **N** (No) beside each question completion.
Have you ever:

_____ spent money to impress someone?

_____ put more food on your plate than you could eat?

_____ wished you had something you couldn't afford?

_____ bought something you didn't need?

_____ been jealous because someone had an item you didn't have?

_____ gone shopping just for the fun of it?

3 Brandi, a seventeen-year-old junior at Central High School, works at a department store after school. She averages fifteen to eighteen hours of work each week. Her parents say she can do whatever she wishes with her income. What would you do with the money, if you were Brandi?

_____

_____

4 What do you think?   **A=AGREE   NS=NOT SURE   D=DISAGREE**

	A	NS	D
a. As Americans, we deserve all we have.	___	___	___
b. People have the right to want to make as much money as they can.	___	___	___
c. People in poorer countries deserve some of what we have.	___	___	___
d. Money is the root of all evil.	___	___	___
e. People should share what they have with others.	___	___	___

	A	NS	D
f. Being rich is a blessing from God.	___	___	___
g. It is sinful to spend a lot of money on yourself for things you don't really need.	___	___	___
h. It is possible to be materialistic without being rich.	___	___	___

5 Read the following scriptures and write out what you think each verse has to say about materialism.

1 Samuel 2:7-8 _____

Mark 8:34-36 _____

Matthew 6:19-21 _____

Psalm 37:7-9 _____

Date Used: _____

Group: _____

MATERIAL WORLD

Topic: Materialism

Purpose of this Session:

This TalkSheet was designed to help young people understand the material world they are living in. The young people of America are growing up in an affluent society. As a result, there is an "affluenza epidemic" among them. They are obsessed with money, both having it and spending it. This session raises a number of important issues concerning money and materialism.

To Introduce the Topic:

Create a master list of all the "things" the students and their families own. Entitle the list "Things" or "Stuff" and display it for all to see. More than likely you will end up with a very long list, to which you can refer later to illustrate how many possessions we American Christians have.

Play a version of a television game show, such as "The Price Is Right", using pictures of expensive items cut from magazines for prizes (stereos, television sets, cars, boats, condo in Hawaii, etc.). Or distribute play money — unevenly, so that some have more than others — and have an auction using the same pictures.

The Discussion:

Item #1: Make a master list of the group's wish list. Have them circle all the things on the wish list that they think they *need* as differentiated from the things they just *want*. This concept is difficult for many to grasp and should be discussed.

Item #2: Try to keep this discussion sensitive in order to move them away from intellectualizing the problems of materialism and poverty. Ask questions such as, "How did it feel when. . .?" Let them express their feelings about the difficulty of living in such a materialistic culture. Talk about what we do with our feelings concerning money and wealth. What do we do with guilt, jealously, pride, etc.?

Item #3: This situation should provoke a good discussion. Should a junior in high school be working fifteen to eighteen hours a week? Should parents be so lenient? Should Brandi's parents make her buy her own clothes and make-up, etc.? Should Brandi tithe to her church?

Item #4: Ask for a vote on each of the statements, according to the way the students answered. If everyone agrees on a particular statement, move on to the next. If there are many different opinions, ask them to defend their points of view. Let them "take a stand" for their positions. Put "strongly agree" on one side of the room, "strongly disagree" on the other with "agree" and "disagree" in the middle. Then have them move to the section corresponding to their vote and debate their choices.

Item #5: Ask some of the students to read aloud their personalized versions of the scriptures. Choose one to discuss more in depth.

To Close the Session:

Ask them to rate themselves on a scale of one to ten — one being *not* materialistic at all, ten being *very* materialistic — as to how materialistic they think they are, without disclosing the results. Challenge them, as followers of Jesus Christ, to change one thing about their lifestyle to make themselves *less* materialistic. Try to help them achieve a lower position on the scale. It would be impossible to move from a "9" to a "0", but very possible to change from a "9" to a "6", then later from a "6" to a "4". This kind of change requires that we begin to change our way of thinking about money, possessions and lifestyle, making difficult decisions in keeping with that which a follower of Jesus Christ would do.

Inform the students the Bible is not neutral on the subject of money. To worship "stuff" is idolatry. A current bumper sticker reads, "When you die, whoever has the most stuff, wins." Nothing could be further from the truth. Happiness and eternal life are not for sale.

Emphasize that receiving comes from giving. God wants us to be givers, not takers. Share Biblical principles concerning giving.

Outside Activites:

1. A Christian service project related to the poor would be appropriate.

2. Have several members of the group make a poster or collage to display, depicting a verse from scripture that discourages materialism, such as Ecclesiastes 5:10.

Watch That Music

1 List three words that best describe music videos.

_____

_____

_____

2 Place an X on the timeline below, nearest the amount of time you spend watching music videos each week.

0 Hours   **10 Hours**   **20 Hours**

3 How do you decide if a particular music video is good or bad?

_____

4 Name five popular music videos and rate them.

TITLE:	DANGEROUS	HARMLESS	GOOD
a. _____	____	____	____
b. _____	____	____	____
c. _____	____	____	____
d. _____	____	____	____
e. _____	____	____	____

5 What do you think?

	That's Right	Sometimes	No Way
a. Music videos don't make much sense to me.	____	____	____
b. Teenagers don't take videos as seriously as parents.	____	____	____
c. Music videos have nothing to do with the song.	____	____	____

	That's Right	Sometimes	No Way
d. Videos exploit women.	____	____	____
e. Parents should watch videos to better understand teenagers.	____	____	____
f. Videos are too violent.	____	____	____
g. Videos are fun to watch.	____	____	____

6 Choose <u>one</u> of the following scriptures to rewrite in your own words:

Galatians 5:13   _____

Ephesians 5:15-17   _____

Colossians 2:8   _____

Philippians 4:8   _____

Date Used: _____

Group: _____

WATCH THAT MUSIC

Topic: Rock music videos

Purpose of this Session:

This TalkSheet is designed to help your students reflect on how much they may be influenced by the rock videos they watch and to evaluate them with their Christian faith in mind.

To Introduce the Session:

If you have access to a video recorder, tape a popular music video and play it for the group. A giant-screen television set would be ideal, as would a sound system that could amplify the sound as loud as they wish. Use discretion when choosing a sampling of rock video. Some are not G-Rated.

The Discussion:

Item #1: Ask the students to share their choices. Make a list for all to see, dividing them into columns marked "Positive" and "Negative" or "Yea" and "Boo".

Item #2: Ask for a show of hands to find out who watches music videos the most and the one who watches the least. Give a special "vidiot award" to the one who watches the most, just for fun.

Item #3: Discuss their ideas and reach a group consensus. You might wish to ask why it is important to be discerning about and to judge something that can be either a good or bad influence.

Item #4: This offers the opportunity to practice what was learned in Item #3. Help them decide if their choices were good, bad or harmless.

Item #5: Have the students literally "take a stand" corresponding to their votes, moving to stand under the appropriate sign in the room — "That's Right" on one side, "No Way" on the other and "Sometimes" in the middle. You may wish to concentrate on the statements "Videos exploit women" and "Videos are too violent" in particular, since these are important issues related to videos. Remember to listen effectively to their opinions. They may have strong opinions on such statements as "Teenagers don't take videos as seriously as parents" and "Videos are fun to watch." Listen to their reasons for believing videos are fun to watch. Try to comprehend their world.

Item #6: Before passing out the TalkSheets, you may wish to assign these passages to different students so all four verses get paraphrased and read to the others. Ask the students to think about how these verses could apply to music videos.

To Close the Session:

Try to maintain a balanced perspective during your conclusion. Too many times we are inclined to summarize a session such as this one in a negative way. This often serves only to turn the young people away from what has been taught. The key issue here is stated in question #2. The main thrust is to decide whether or not a Christian should be watching a particular video.

Another issue is the amount of time spent watching music videos. Ask if that is the best use of their time. Unlike music alone, videos require total attention. There is also the question of imagination. Ask if rock videos are replacing the gift of creative imagination and individual interpretation. Music videos are programmed to interpret a song for us, i.e., to think for us. Is this good or bad?

There are now many outstanding Christian rock videos available, for sale or for rent. If possible, show one of these to the students.

Outside Activities:

1. Suggest the students watch a rock music video with their parents. The point will be for them to discuss the meaning of the video with their parents and report the results.

2. After viewing a Christian music video (available from your local Christian bookstore), compare it to the secular ones.

TRUST ME

1 "Never trust anyone over thirty" was a slogan popular in the 1960's. How would you re-write that slogan today?

"Never trust anyone _____."

2 Name a person you trust completely and state why you do. _____
_____

3 Think of a person you do not trust. Why do you not trust this person? _____
_____

4 Complete this sentence:

If I had a friend who double-crossed me or lied about me behind my back, I would _____
_____

5 Answer each of the following questions by placing an X on the line at the point best describing you.

How much can your parents trust you?

Totally _____ **Not at all**

How much can your teachers trust you?

Totally _____ **Not at all**

How much can your friends trust you?

Totally _____ **Not at all**

6 What do you think?

	AGREE	DISAGREE		AGREE	DISAGREE
a. Overall, the average person can be trusted.	____	____	**d.** Once a person betrays your trust, it is impossible to trust them completely ever again.	____	____
b. It is easier to trust Christians than non-Christians.	____	____	**e.** It is safer not to trust anyone.	____	____
c. I have difficulty trusting people.	____	____			

7 Study one of the following passages of scripture and be prepared to discuss it.

Psalm 52:8-9   **Proverbs 3:5-6**   **Leviticus 6:2-5**

Date Used: _____

Group: _____

TRUST ME

Topic: Trust

Purpose of this Session:

Early adolescence often brings the first experiences of betrayal. Young people learn there are some people who cannot be trusted. But what of the Christian and trust? How much trust should Christians extend to each other and how trustworthy should Christians be?

To Introduce the Topic:

Divide the group into couples, with one person in each pair keeping their eyes closed on a "blind walk". The couples walk around the church property, the seeing person responsible for the safety of the other. Have them reverse roles and repeat the experiment. Discuss whether or not it was difficult to trust one another and how the seeing person helped or hindered the "blind" partner.

The Discussion:

Item #1: Share the students' new slogans. Encourage them to be creative. You might want to contribute a couple of your own, to get things started. Humor is allowed: "Never trust anyone who tries to pay back a loan with Monopoly money." Some responses will be in a serious vein. Ask for explanations.

Regarding the slogan about trusting people over the age of thirty, you may want to ask, "Why do you think young people in the sixties had trouble trusting adults?" and "Do you have trouble trusting adults today?"

Item #2: Have the group share the names they chose and ask them why they put their trust in these people.

Item #3: Do not permit any specific names to be mentioned here, unless the untrustworthy person is universally notorious. Instead, ask them to share only the characteristics of the people indicating their untrustworthiness.

Item #4: Nearly all of the students will have had a friend who has betrayed a confidence in some way. Let them share their experiences as long as they do not use names or talk about anyone in the group. Ask if they learned anything from the experience and if they double-crossed their friend in return.

Item #5: Ask for a show of hands indicating their opinions on these questions. If there is a strong disagreement on any, have a debate on the issue, and ask them to share any strong feelings they might have. Discuss how a person can earn the trust of someone else and how much trust you should extend to a person you don't know very well.

Item #6: Relate these scriptures to trusting relationships today. Focus particularly on the fact that we can trust God no matter what. God will never disappoint us or let us down.

To Close the Session:

Challenge the students to be trustworthy. They will not always be able to trust everyone but they, themselves, can be trustworthy. Trust must be earned and developed over time. No one automatically deserves to be trusted. Trust is a treasure and an asset. Once it is tarnished, it is difficult to restore to its original luster. They should not be surprised if their parents or their friends don't trust them once they have been untrustworthy. There is an old saying that goes, "There's only one thing finer than having a friend you can trust; being trustworthy yourself."

Outside Activities:

1. Ask the group to interview adult members of the congregation regarding trust, making up their own questions, and have them report their findings.

2. Ask the students to watch television for a couple of hours, making a list of the people on a program or in a commercial. Rate them on a scale of 1 to 10, according to how trustworthy they seem. Are they believable? Are they telling the truth?

3. Assign a search of the scriptures for examples of trust and mistrust, sharing the results with the group.

OH, GOD

1 What is the first word that comes to mind when you think about God? _____

_____

_____

2 Why do you believe in God? Don't use the Bible as proof; pretend the question comes from someone who doesn't believe the Bible is true. _____

_____

_____

3 If you could ask God any question, knowing He would answer, what would it be? _____

_____

_____

4 If God wrote you a personal letter, what would He say to you?

Dear _____

_____

_____

_____

_____

**Sincerely,
God**

5 Brian has always felt there was a God, but he has never really felt close to Him or felt God really cared about him. See if you can give Brian some suggestions as to how he can get to know God better.

_____

_____

_____

6 Choose one or more of the following statements that best describes your relationship with God.

a. I have a personal relationship with God. _____

b. I feel very far away from God. _____

c. I want to become closer to God. _____

d. My relationship with God is my number-one priority. _____

e. I believe God is pleased with the way I live my life. _____

f. I don't believe anyone can have a close relationship with God. _____

g. I still have a lot of doubts about God. _____

h. I know God loves me and cares about me. _____

7 Read Romans 11:33-36. What do these verses have to say about God? _____

_____

Date Used: _____

Group: _____

OH, GOD

Topic: God

Purpose of this Session:

This TalkSheet was designed to create a discussion among the young people about their reasons for believing in God, what He is like, and how their belief makes a difference in the way they live.

To Introduce the Session:

Divide the students into small groups and tell them they are "advertising agencies" assigned to create a thirty-second commercial for God, which is going to be on national televison during prime time. They need to "sell" God to the world. Allow enough time for them to make up their skits before they present them to each other.

An alternative would be to have an "atheist" speak to the group. He or she can give a short talk on why there is no God and why atheism is the "only" intelligent point of view. Invite an actual atheist or have someone unknown to the group impersonate one.

The Discussion:

Item #1: On the blackboard or overhead projector, list all the words suggested. Explain how unfortunate it is that many have the wrong idea about God. They may think of him as a "cosmic cop", or an old bearded man, or a heavenly Santa Claus. We need to develop a healthy, Biblical image of God.

Item #2: Play the devil's advocate and press the students to think of reasons that make sense. Challenge them a little bit. You may want to ask how they would change the way they live, if they knew for certain there was no God.

Item #3: Have the students share their questions, but don't try to answer them now, unless you feel it necessary. You might ask different ones to play the part of "God" and to attempt to answer the question. Reassure them it is normal to have a lot of questions we would like to ask God. They should pray and ask God to help them discover the answers. We may not get a satisfactory answer to some questions now, but we'll get a chance to ask God face-to-face someday.

Item #4: Ask for volunteers to share their letters and what they might have learned from this exercise. Emphasize God does speak to us and we need to listen to Him more. He has also written to us, using His word, the Bible. God has a personal message for each one of us in the Bible. If we believe in God, then we must also believe what he has to say to us is important.

Item #5: Use this "Tension Getter" to discuss practical ways to have a better relationship with God. Make a master list of all the suggestions they come up with. You may want to add some of your own. Tell the students to choose the three they think are the best and to select one of those to do this week.

Item #6: Ask for volunteers to share their responses. Encourage those who sincerely wish a deeper, closer relationship with God.

Item #7: Use this scripture to focus on several of the attributes of God.

To Close the Session:

A moment of prayer — talking to God — would be appropriate to close this session. Ask the students to pray in short sentences, telling God what they have learned about Him.

Another way to close would be to present a short message on "What God Thinks of You." Emphasize that God thinks they are great — He loves them, in fact. He knows their names, their problems, their worries. He wants all of us to experience an abundant, happy life. That's why he sent His Son to die for us on the Cross.

Help the students understand if they say they believe in God, then their lives need to be representative of that statement. They need to become more "godly" in their day-to-day living.

Other Activities:

1. Have the group members select several Psalms to study. Afterward, they should be able to write down five things they learned about God, reporting back to the group what they learned that was new to them.

2. Ask the students to watch for "evidence" of God's presence in the world during the next week and report back where they saw God and were they did *not* see God.

I WONDER

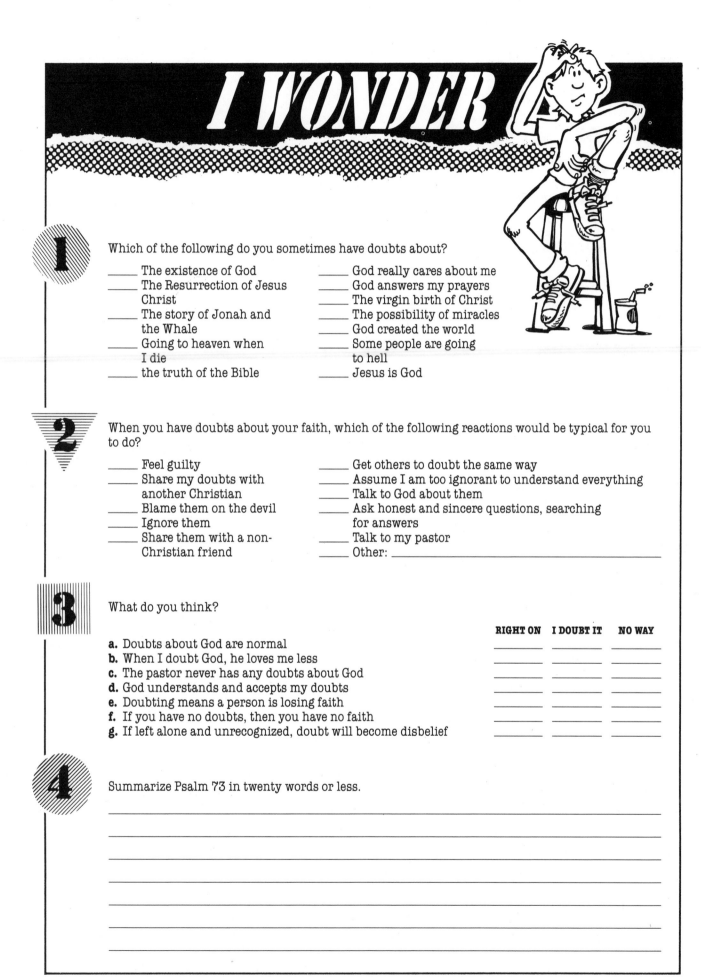

1 Which of the following do you sometimes have doubts about?

_____ The existence of God
_____ The Resurrection of Jesus Christ
_____ The story of Jonah and the Whale
_____ Going to heaven when I die
_____ the truth of the Bible

_____ God really cares about me
_____ God answers my prayers
_____ The virgin birth of Christ
_____ The possibility of miracles
_____ God created the world
_____ Some people are going to hell
_____ Jesus is God

2 When you have doubts about your faith, which of the following reactions would be typical for you to do?

_____ Feel guilty
_____ Share my doubts with another Christian
_____ Blame them on the devil
_____ Ignore them
_____ Share them with a non-Christian friend

_____ Get others to doubt the same way
_____ Assume I am too ignorant to understand everything
_____ Talk to God about them
_____ Ask honest and sincere questions, searching for answers
_____ Talk to my pastor
_____ Other: _____

3 What do you think?

	RIGHT ON	I DOUBT IT	NO WAY
a. Doubts about God are normal	_____	_____	_____
b. When I doubt God, he loves me less	_____	_____	_____
c. The pastor never has any doubts about God	_____	_____	_____
d. God understands and accepts my doubts	_____	_____	_____
e. Doubting means a person is losing faith	_____	_____	_____
f. If you have no doubts, then you have no faith	_____	_____	_____
g. If left alone and unrecognized, doubt will become disbelief	_____	_____	_____

4 Summarize Psalm 73 in twenty words or less.

_____
_____
_____
_____
_____
_____
_____
_____

Date Used: _____

Group: _____

I WONDER

Topic: Doubt

Purpose of this Session:

Doubt and skepticism are normal, even healthy, in young people. If they are ever to have a strong faith of their own, they must go through a period of doubt and, perhaps, even disbelief. Therefore, it is vitally important they be able to discuss their confusion with responsible adults such as yourself. This TalkSheet offers the opportunity to discuss these doubts.

To Introduce the Topic:

It would be effective to give a fabricated personal testimony. Pretend, in a testimonial, you have lost your faith and are considering giving up Christianity. Inform one of the students or another adult of your plan and ask them to query you with soul-searching questions. End the farce by walking out of the room in disbelief.

Another way is to share some of the doubts you had when younger and some you may have now, but remember not to overwhelm the students with too much dubiousness. Tension is fine, but too much can be overly confusing.

The Discussion:

Item #1: Insist on honesty, even though it might be very difficult for them to admit they have doubts. Find out which statement created the most doubt. If no one expresses any doubt, ask them why they are so positive.

Resist providing all the "right" answers. Do not try to eliminate all their doubt with quick answers. Young people who are subjected to constant spiritual rescue with right answers have more difficulty when faced with situations that test their faith. If you detect a great deal of doubt on any of these issues, make a note to discuss them later, in more depth.

Item #2: The point of this exercise is to discover what *should* be done when doubt is present. Ask for a vote to decide which are "good" and which are "bad".

Item #3: Ask the group to share their opinions on these statements and make it clear to them that doubt is normal for everyone, even pastors. Reinforce the fact that God will not reject us or love us less for doubting. Doubt is almost a prerequisite for developing a strong faith; no faith is required if you are absolutely sure about something. Knowing we are alive does not demand any faith. It is an established fact and there is no doubt about it.

Item #4: This is a beautifully written Psalm about doubt. Ask for a sharing of the students' summaries, perhaps having them work on their ideas in smaller groups, combining their ideas.

To Close the Session:

Tell the story of John the Baptist and how he confidently announced the coming of Christ, then, when he was thrown into prison, began to have doubts about whether Jesus actually was the Son of God or not (Luke 7:18-23). Help the students lose their fear of doubting, reiterating that doubt is normal. An absolute acceptance of everything taught is not necessary to a successfully Christian life. Having doubt does not mean the loss of faith nor that the doubter has sinned. The Christian writer Frederick Buechner said, "Doubt is the ants in the pants of faith; it keeps it alive and moving." Doubt stimulates closer growth toward God. Challenge them to search for a deeper, more meaningful faith and encourage them to talk to people who trust and care about them. Talking with parents or other responsible, respected adults can strengthen and deepen their faith in Jesus Christ.

Impart this additional quote to the group: "Doubt your doubts, just like you would doubt your faith." Doubts themselves are not absolute nor final.

Finally, suggest they save their "big doubts" for God Himself because they may never be answered in this life. We may not have all the answers, but God does. As I Corinthians 13:12 says, "Now we see through a glass darkly, but someday, we will see face to face." God will reveal all truth to us.

Outside Activities:

Ask the members of the group to interview select members of the congregation as to any doubts they might have had about Christianity, and then to share the results.

Jesus Giveaway

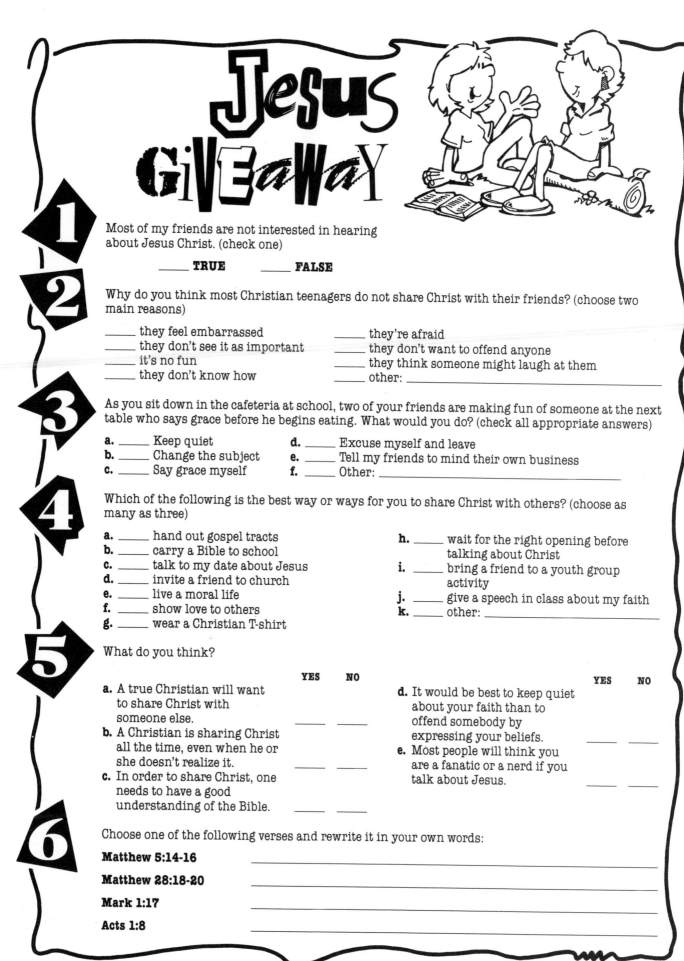

1 Most of my friends are not interested in hearing about Jesus Christ. (check one)

_____ **TRUE**   _____ **FALSE**

2 Why do you think most Christian teenagers do not share Christ with their friends? (choose two main reasons)

_____ they feel embarrassed
_____ they don't see it as important
_____ it's no fun
_____ they don't know how

_____ they're afraid
_____ they don't want to offend anyone
_____ they think someone might laugh at them
_____ other: _____

3 As you sit down in the cafeteria at school, two of your friends are making fun of someone at the next table who says grace before he begins eating. What would you do? (check all appropriate answers)

a. _____ Keep quiet
b. _____ Change the subject
c. _____ Say grace myself

d. _____ Excuse myself and leave
e. _____ Tell my friends to mind their own business
f. _____ Other: _____

4 Which of the following is the best way or ways for you to share Christ with others? (choose as many as three)

a. _____ hand out gospel tracts
b. _____ carry a Bible to school
c. _____ talk to my date about Jesus
d. _____ invite a friend to church
e. _____ live a moral life
f. _____ show love to others
g. _____ wear a Christian T-shirt

h. _____ wait for the right opening before talking about Christ
i. _____ bring a friend to a youth group activity
j. _____ give a speech in class about my faith
k. _____ other: _____

5 What do you think?

	YES	NO		YES	NO
a. A true Christian will want to share Christ with someone else.	_____	_____	**d.** It would be best to keep quiet about your faith than to offend somebody by expressing your beliefs.	_____	_____
b. A Christian is sharing Christ all the time, even when he or she doesn't realize it.	_____	_____	**e.** Most people will think you are a fanatic or a nerd if you talk about Jesus.	_____	_____
c. In order to share Christ, one needs to have a good understanding of the Bible.	_____	_____			

6 Choose one of the following verses and rewrite it in your own words:

Matthew 5:14-16 _____

Matthew 28:18-20 _____

Mark 1:17 _____

Acts 1:8 _____

Date Used: _____

Group: _____

JESUS GIVEAWAY

Topic: Sharing Christ with others; witnessing

Purpose of this Session:

Even some adults find it difficult to share their faith in Christ, so it should come as no surprise that young people have the same trouble. This TalkSheet was designed to give you the opportunity to discuss with your group why it is so tough to share Christ with others and to explore effective ways to witness for Christ.

To Introduce the Topic:

Ask your group to pretend English-speaking aliens from outer space have landed on our planet. Have several volunteers role-play a situation in which they try to share their Christian faith with these beings who have never heard one word about Jesus Christ before.

The Discussion:

Item #1: Many in the group will say the statement is true — their friends are not interested in hearing about Christ. Ask them to explain their answers. Anticipate their having difficulty with the explanations.

Item #2: Try to have the group reach a consensus as to which are the top two reasons. Ask if they are valid or not. Discuss ways of overcoming each of these obstacles.

Item #3: This "Tension Getter" will give the students a chance to experience a situation in which they can share their faith. Have three people role-play the plot and ask them to act it out the way they think it would actually occur. You might role-play it several times, using different approaches.

Item #4: Have the students share their answers and the reasons why they responded that way. Debate the pros and cons of each of the methods listed. Ask if anyone has used any of these methods, with success or without.

Item #5: Discuss these statements one at a time. Find out what the group decides as a whole. Help them understand (1) a true Christian will want to tell others about Christ, (2) we are representing Christ by the way we live, (3) it isn't necessary to know the Bible in order to share Christ, (4) it's copping-out to think we might be offensive if we share Christ and (5) we shouldn't be worried about what people think of us when sharing Christ. It isn't necessary to be superbly articulate when sharing; the *desire* to do so is more important. We do not have to *talk* about Christ in order to share the Christian way of living and we do not have to be perfect. If we share Christ out of love and in an appropriate manner, it is doubtful anyone would be offended. It is helpful to remember some of the most admired people in the world are strong Christians and outspoken about being so.

Item #6: In reviewing these scriptures, examine the different methods Christ used to talk about Himself and how these same methods can be used today to share Christ, such as friendship, helping others, etc.

To Close the Session:

Using some of the ideas that surfaced during the discussion plus any of your own, help the students see they can share Christ with their friends. It isn't necessary to be a Biblical scholar to talk about Christ. Someone once said, "Sharing Christ is basically one hungry beggar telling another where he found food." Encourage them to share their faith as Christ commanded His followers to do. Review the different ways for sharing faith and request they try earnestly to put these methods into practice during their lives for the coming week.

Outside Activities:

1. Ask the students to choose one friend with whom they will share Christ this week. They could also pray for another group member as the latter shares Christ with a friend.

2. Organize an outreach program with your youth group. brainstorm a few ideas for reaching new students or new neighbors for Christ, such as promoting a Christian concert, having an evangelistic social event, putting an ad in the school newspaper for a youth group event, or doing a service project in the community which gives the group members a chance to share their faith with others.

Are You Talking About Me?

1 Pretend your picture is in the local newspaper. What does the article say about you? _____

_____

2 Place an **X** on the scale lines below at the point that best describes how you are feeling about yourself.

out of place	like I belong		worthless	worthwhile

loved	unwanted		attractive	ugly

stupid	smart		superior	inferior

important	insignificant		capable	incompetent

3 Complete this sentence: "I am proud of _____

_____"

4 What do you think?   M=THAT'S ME   N=THAT'S NOT ME

	M	N			M	N
a. I never feel satisfied with what I have done.	☐	☐	**f.** I think I am below average.		☐	☐
b. I put myself down more than I build myself up.	☐	☐	**g.** I want to be liked so badly I do things I shouldn't do in order to be accepted.		☐	☐
c. I can accept the compliments of others.	☐	☐	**h.** When I meet someone new, I worry about their liking me.		☐	☐
d. I feel inferior around people my age.	☐	☐	**i.** I depend on what others say to make me feel important.		☐	☐
e. I cannot take criticism well.	☐	☐				

5 Herman has a nose the size of a banana. People have been making fun of the way he looks for so long, he believes them. Herman now puts himself down more than other people do.

How would you treat Herman? _____

_____

What could you do to make him feel better about himself? _____

_____

What could you say to him when he puts himself down? _____

_____

6 Read the following scriptures to discover how God sees you.

Psalm 139:13-18   Luke 16:15   Ephesians 2:10
Psalm 147:10-11   2 Corinthians 5:17-18

ARE YOU TALKING ABOUT ME?

Topic: Self-image and self-esteem

Purpose of this Session:

This TalkSheet was designed to give your youth group the opportunity to discuss their self-image or self-esteem. The way each of us sees ourselves has a profound effect on our emotional and spiritual development. A healthy self-image and good feelings about our worthiness are things we all want to see in ourselves and in our young people.

To Introduce the Session:

Have a "Compliment Contest", asking two students to stand up and try to compliment each other more than the other. The rest of the group can vote on the winner. This can be fun as well as a positive, affirming experience for them, so let several pairs of students have a turn.

Another way is to distribute blank sheets of typing paper and straight pins, having everyone pin one to their backs. Each person writes one thing they like about the others on the sheet of paper. Allow time for the students to remove and read their paper signs. Discuss how they felt as a result.

The Discussion:

Item #1: Ask for volunteers to read their "press release". If no one wishes to volunteer, do not insist. Ask for a show of hands indicating how many wrote "positive" stories and how many wrote "negative" ones.

Item #2: The answers to this exercise are not to be shared with the group. Instead, ask if this was difficult or easy, if a certain one was more difficult than another and if, afterward, they felt better or worse.

How young people feel about themselves is often determined by how they think others view them. The feelings listed are frequently the result of others' perceptions rather than a realistic assessment. Tell the students God sees them differently than their peers do. They need to know they can have some control over how they see themselves rather than allowing others to control their self-esteem. Ask them to re-examine their positions on the line scales and to decide how much the opinions of others has affected their view of themselves.

Item #3: Encourage some bragging here, because everyone has *something* they are proud of. Most of them will probably mention a material possession or something other than a personal quality. Insist they think of something they can be proud of. Many will discount a positive attribute with an immediate apology or put-down. Help them understand pride in themselves is a healthy trait.

Another way to approach this exercise is to have each person stand, one at a time, and then ask the others in the group to enumerate the things they would be proud of *if they were that person*. The one who is "it" will probably be pleased and surprised at how many things they can be proud of and didn't realize they had.

Item #4: Discuss each issue in general terms without asking for their individual answers. You might ask the students to answer impersonally, as if they were "a typical high school student". They may open up more if you share how you felt about yourself as a teenager.

Item #5: This "Tension Getter" gives you a chance to talk about ministering to others as regards self-esteem. Allow each person to state how they would respond to Herman. Put-downs are a common self-protective defense method among teenagers and have a strongly adverse effect on self-esteem.

Item #6: Ask volunteers to read these passages of scripture aloud, then ask the group to focus on how God sees us and if this makes any difference to them.

To Close the Session:

It is important for the students to realize feelings of inadequacy are normal. Everone, even famous celebrities who seem outwardly self-confident, have feelings of inadequacy and fear of failure. Challenge them to try to see themselves as God sees them — children of God, created in the image of God. They can take control of their own self-esteem rather than allow the perceptions of others to affect them.

Each young person in the group has the potential to become all they want to be, if they will allow God to take control of their lives. Biblical examples include Moses, who had a speech impediment and Paul, who apparently was not very handsome and had a "thorn in the flesh". If we keep putting ourselves down, God cannot use us.

Emphasize that many times we have a low self-image because we become preoccupied with ourselves. Television and motion pictures cater to this by making us feel inferior because our lives are not as exciting and glamorous as those of celebrities. This is a trap. The best way to stop thinking negatively about ourselves is to stop being self-centered and to begin putting others first. If we care about and serve others, our self-image will become more positive.

God created us in His image. He loves and cares about us and even died for us. For that reason alone we need to have a high regard for ourselves. "God don't make junk."

Outside Activities:

Ask the students to keep a daily journal about their self-image for a week and share what they learned with the group.

YOUTH GROUP

1 Complete this sentence: "The best thing about this youth group is _____ _____ _____ _____."

2 List three words that best describe our youth group. _____ _____ _____

3 Suppose you buried a time capsule filled with things representing your youth group. What would you decide is important enough to be included?

_____
_____
_____

4 Pretend you are an adult youth leader working with this youth group. What would you do differently from what is being done now?

_____
_____
_____

5 What do you think?   **!**=RIGHT ON   **?**=NOT SURE   **X**=NO WAY

a. Our youth group discussions and activities influence me a great deal. ____

b. Our youth group has good leaders. ____

c. This youth group is Christ-centered. ____

d. I feel like I am an important part of the group. ____

e. I attend mostly because my parents make me. ____

f. I am doing my part to help make this a better group. ____

g. I would be comfortable inviting friends at school to visit this group. ____

h. This group has helped me grow in my relationship to Christ. ____

i. I give this group high priority in my life. ____

j. I have a lot of good friends in this group. ____

6 Read **Ephesians 4:1-6**, then write a postcard addressed to your youth group explaining what you learned and how it can improve the group.

Date Used: _____

Group: _____

MY YOUTH GROUP

Topic: Evaluation of your youth group

Purpose of this Session:

Students often take their youth group for granted. When things are going great, they enjoy it. When they aren't so great, they complain. This TalkSheet gives you an opportunity to assess the youth group in a positive way. It can also be used separately, with the youth leaders, as a helpful planning tool.

To Introduce the Session:

There are several approaches you can use to begin talking about the health and condition of your youth group. Whatever you choose, remember to keep the conversation upbeat and positive. You do not want it to turn into a what's-wrong-with-our-group gripe session. Suggest the students describe other groups they have been members of or have visited. This will illustrate no group is perfect.

Another possibility is to ask the members to give imitations of adult leaders trying to lead a youth group function. This can be hilarious and you may learn a thing or two about yourself. Another way is to have adult leaders share what the group means to them.

The Discussion:

Item #1: This incomplete sentence starts things off on a positive note. Mention you hope to keep the discussion helpful and affirmative. Don't be afraid to interrupt the discussion if it becomes too negative and full of put-downs.

Item #2: Ask the students to share the words they chose, placing them on the board if you wish, in two separate columns marked "Negative" and "Positive" or "Yea" and "Boo".

Item #3: List the items chosen and discuss why these were important. Discuss items they chose *not* to put in the time capsule. Beforehand, if possible, ask some of the adults in the church to list items they would have buried in a time capsule during their youth group days and share these with your group.

Item #4: This exercise will offer you the opportunity to discuss what it is like to be a youth worker. Have the students describe what they would do differently if they were one of the leaders. Don't allow this to become a put-down session, but strive for a positive brainstorming to seek ways the group can be improved. Ask other "If you were a youth leader" questions, such as: "What is the most frustrating part of your job?", "What is the most rewarding part?" and "What are your goals?"

Item #5: Ask for volunteers to share their responses. Not everyone will want to. You may want to collect these TalkSheets to help you evaluate how the students feel about the group. Tell them in advance not to put their names on the sheets.

Item #6: Have volunteers share their postcards, based upon the scripture.

To Close the Session:

Close with a postitive affirmation of everyone in the group. Let them know they are important; without them there wouldn't be a group to discuss, and that their comments and concerns are going to be taken seriously. This might be a good time to invite them to take a more active role, to get more involved. It would also be appropriate to close with a prayer, allowing the students to pray for the group and its leaders.

Outside Activities:

Have a planning session during which the students can help contribute ideas for activities and programs for the coming year. A good resource for this is *The Youth Group Planning Calendar* by David Lynn (Youth Specialties, 1224 Greenfield Drive, El Cajon, CA 92021).

THE HEAT IS ON

1 Complete the following sentence: "If I could change one thing about my life, I would _____

_____

_____."

2 Below is a list of possible teenage problems. Check three you think are the most common:

- ☐ **Not having a job**
- ☐ **Being spiritually down**
- ☐ **Being pressured to begin dating**
- ☐ **Having health problems**
- ☐ **Getting bad grades**
- ☐ **Having a poor self-image**

- ☐ **Doing drugs**
- ☐ **Not having enough friends**
- ☐ **Being bored**
- ☐ **Worrying about divorce of parents**
- ☐ **Having sex problems**

- ☐ **Being in trouble with the law**
- ☐ **Being depressed**
- ☐ **Not having a car**
- ☐ **Having parents that are too strict**
- ☐ **Other:** _____

3 Place an **X** on the line scale below that best denotes the number of problems you are having in your life.

I am having more problems than most people my age

I am having fewer problems than most people my age

4 What do you think? SA=STRONGLY AGREE   A=AGREE
D=DISAGREE   SD=STRONGLY DISAGREE

a. _____ Problems are normal and to be expected.

b. _____ I believe most of the problems I have will solve themselves.

c. _____ What I do today will determine what happens tomorrow.

d. _____ Many times it is useless to try and make things better.

e. _____ God cares about every problem I have.

f. _____ I have difficulty deciding what to do when I have big problems.

g. _____ When bad things happen, there is nothing I can do about them.

h. _____ Christians have fewer problems than non-Christians.

i. _____ I feel far away from God when I am having problems.

j. _____ I am able to talk to someone about my problems.

5 Choose one of the following scriptures to rewrite in your own words.

Proverbs 19:20-21   **1 Thessalonians 5:18**   **Romans 5:3-5**   **2 Corinthians 1:3-5**

_____

_____

_____

_____

THE HEAT IS ON

Topic: Teen Problems

Purpose of this Session:

Each stage of life presents its own unique problems. Adolesence is no exception. Unlike adults, however, teenagers have not had experience in dealing with problems. This creates stress and depression in many young people of today. This TalkSheet was designed to give you the chance to talk about problems, how Christians deal with them and how to solve them.

To Introduce the Session:

Collect a few "Dear Ann Landers" or "Dear Abby" columns from your newspaper and read a few of the "problems" to the group. Let them come up with an solution. See if theirs is different from the advice given by the columnist.

Another opener is to have each person anonymously write down their biggest problem. Collect and screen the problems, choosing several to solve with the group. Have volunteers read them and pretend the problems are theirs. Encourage the use of scripture as they ask the group to help find a solution. The person who actually has the problem receives help without having to reveal his or her identity. This is a good lead for discussing problems.

The Discussion:

Item #1: Make a master list of all the changes your students would like. Decide which they have control over and which they do not.

Item #2: Ask for a vote on these problems and see which ones are considered the worst. Ask why they believe these are such big problems for young people and if they can come up with any solutions.

Item #3: Copy the scale line from #3 on the board, overhead projector or newsprint and ask where they would place the X for minority youth, handicapped youth, Third World youth, etc. Let them understand they are not the only ones with problems.

Item #4: These statements give you an opportunity to talk about a Christian perspective in problem solving. Emphasize taking responsibility instead of making excuses. Let them know the patterns learned and applied now toward solving problems will follow them for a lifetime. Encourage them to avoid procrastination and to take charge. The last item on the list deals with talking to someone about problems. Ask "If you had a problem with _____, who would seek advice from?" Encourage them to seek advice from others and let them know you are always available to help.

Item #5: These scriptures look at problems from different perspectives. Ask several of the students to read what they have written.

To Close the Session:

The story of David and Goliath is appropriate for closing the session. Goliath represented a very big problem for David. There were people who probably said to David, "David, the giant is so big, there is no way you can win!" But David's attitude, as he loaded his sling, was, "No, the giant is so big, there's no way I can miss!" Even the biggest problem can become an opportunity to grow and become a winner.

Tell the students problems are normal, even the difficult ones that seem to be unique to them. A bigger problem is not having the experience and maturity to know how to solve them. That's where we come in. We want to be a resource for them.

Encourage your young people to talk their problems over with their parents. If this seems impossible to them, emphasize how important it is for them to seek out a responsible adult like yourself, the pastor or their school counselor.

Challenge them to consider each problem from God's perspective. Very often, scripture will tell us what to do or how to deal with a particular problem. Challenge them to seek God's help through prayer, because God cares and understands.

Outside Activities:

1. Have a "Dear Gabby" box in which the students can place their questions and concerns. Cut a slit in the top of a shoe box and place 3x5 cards and pencils nearby or pass them out at the end of the meeting. Answer the questions the following week or let the group answer them.

2. One good way to help a person deal with their own problems is to help someone else with theirs. Plan a service project that focuses on the problems of others.

3. Ask the group to bring news articles related to problems other people are having and discuss them. This will help the students move away from an egocentric perspective.

ROCK ON

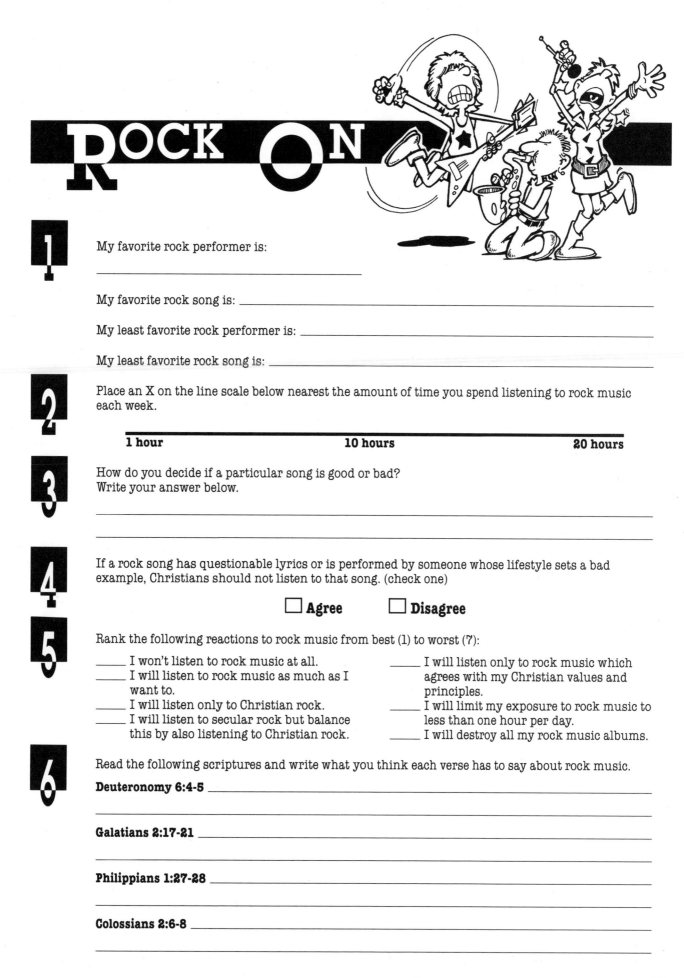

1

My favorite rock performer is:

_____

My favorite rock song is: _____

My least favorite rock performer is: _____

My least favorite rock song is: _____

2

Place an X on the line scale below nearest the amount of time you spend listening to rock music each week.

1 hour	10 hours	20 hours

3

How do you decide if a particular song is good or bad?
Write your answer below.

_____

_____

4

If a rock song has questionable lyrics or is performed by someone whose lifestyle sets a bad example, Christians should not listen to that song. (check one)

☐ **Agree**   ☐ **Disagree**

5

Rank the following reactions to rock music from best (1) to worst (7):

_____ I won't listen to rock music at all.
_____ I will listen to rock music as much as I want to.
_____ I will listen only to Christian rock.
_____ I will listen to secular rock but balance this by also listening to Christian rock.

_____ I will listen only to rock music which agrees with my Christian values and principles.
_____ I will limit my exposure to rock music to less than one hour per day.
_____ I will destroy all my rock music albums.

6

Read the following scriptures and write what you think each verse has to say about rock music.

Deuteronomy 6:4-5 _____

_____

Galatians 2:17-21 _____

_____

Philippians 1:27-28 _____

_____

Colossians 2:6-8 _____

_____

Date Used: _____

Group: _____

ROCK ON

Topic: Rock-n-Roll music

Purpose of this Session:

Rock music often divides young people and adults in the church. With rare exceptions, teenagers — Christian teenagers included — listen to and are influenced by rock music. This TalkSheet is designed to facilitate a balanced discussion about this kind of music.

To Introduce the Session:

Invite the members of the group to bring their favorite albums and tapes to the meeting and listen to them together. They like their music played loudly and you may want to indulge them to help you and them better understand the kind of music that permeates their culture.

It is important to introduce the session in a positive way. Don't bad-mouth rock music in the beginning, making the discussion one-sided. Include some secular rock music — or jazz — that you enjoy, even if it is twenty years old. Most of today's young people are familiar with the hits of the '50s, '60s and '70s. Try to attain an atmosphere of fun, learning and openness as you get into this discussion.

The Discussion:

Item #1: Have fun with this. Let the kids lobby and vote for whomever they think is the best peformer and the best song.

Item #2: Find out when your students listen to rock music — before school, during lunch, only on weekends, etc. Compare how much time they spend listening with how much time they spend on other things, such as watching television, working, family activities, Bible study, prayer, etc.

Item #3: Reach a consensus of all their ideas on this exercise. You might want to ask why it is important or not to judge whether something is good or bad for them. This activity can help teach young people they need to evaluate the songs they listen to, even though they may be considered very popular by their culture. This would be a good time to evaluate some of the songs that were mentioned in Item #1, in light of the criteria they suggest here. Ask if they are good or bad when judged according to these standards.

Item #4: Expect some heated opinions in reaction to this statement. If time allows, display some of the teen magazines that feature rock stars, such as *Tiger Beat*. Magazines such as this have pictures and interviews with rock stars and will give you a lot of material for discussion.

Item #5: Allow for a debate on this activity. See if your group can arrive at a consensus that would have a good GA (God Approved) rating.

Item #6: Ask several students to share what they believe these scriptures say about rock music.

To Close the Session:

Rock music, as a style, is no more of an evil in and of itself than bluegrass or classical music. To try and convince young people otherwise is not only wrong, but foolish. What is important is to help them choose the kind of rock music they are going to listen to. It isn't wrong to like music with a rock beat, but it is wrong for Christians to spend time and money embracing anything that undermines the values of the kingdom of God, whether it is rock music or anything else.

Good questions to ask are, "When you listen to a rock song, does it draw you closer to God or farther away from God?" and "Does it reflect values consistent with the Christian faith or those which are opposed to it?" Rock music, like many other things in life, is not neutral. It can have an effect upon the listeners, good and bad.

Take this time to share your own opinions about rock music, but do it with respect for others' feelings. This would be a good time to introduce the group to good Christian rock music, especially if they aren't familiar with some of the more popular artists. Listen to some together and ask their opinion of it. If you are not familiar with what is going on in the field of Christian rock, visit a Christian bookstore and ask what is available.

Outside Activities:

1. Have the group study the "Top 40" list of current hard rock hits and rate each song according to the content of the lyrics, the lifestyles of the artists, the music itself and any other criteria desired. List them from "best" to "worst", creating a new "Youth Group Top 40" which can be copied and distributed to the members and sent to the radio stations in your area.

2. Menconi Ministries (P.O. Box 306, Cardiff-by-the-Sea, CA 92007-0831) provides videos, tapes and other materials about rock music which can be used for further discussion. Menconi also publishes the "Hot 200", which provides short profiles of current rock artists.

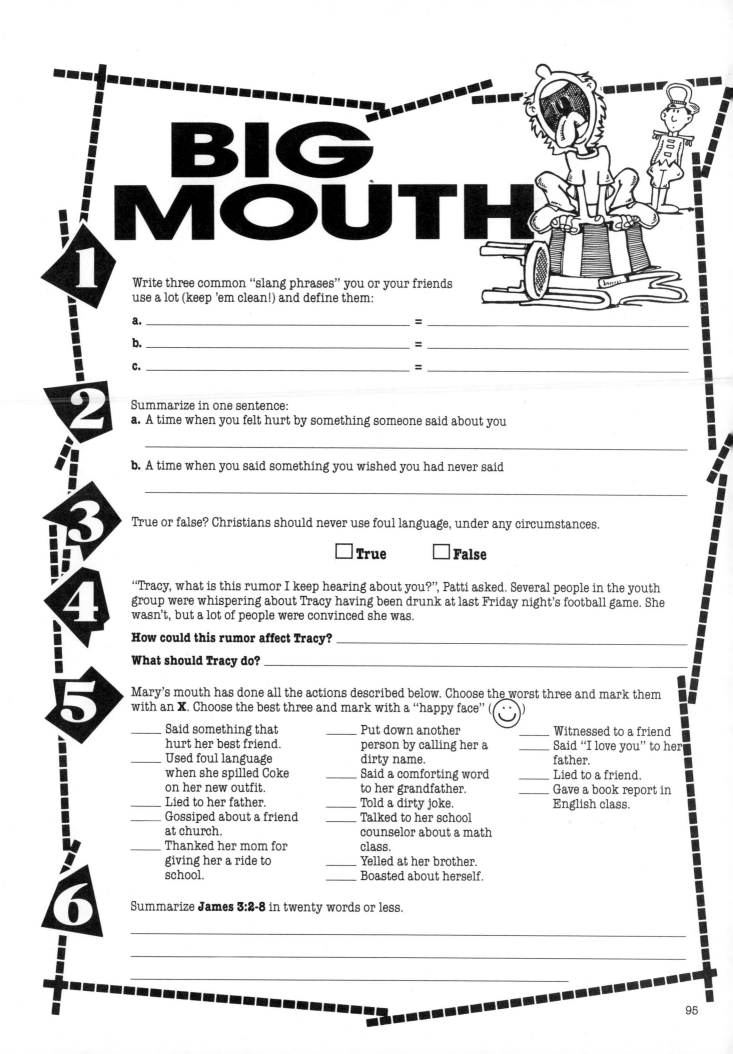

BIG MOUTH

1 Write three common "slang phrases" you or your friends use a lot (keep 'em clean!) and define them:

a. _____ = _____

b. _____ = _____

c. _____ = _____

2 Summarize in one sentence:

a. A time when you felt hurt by something someone said about you

_____

b. A time when you said something you wished you had never said

_____

3 True or false? Christians should never use foul language, under any circumstances.

☐ **True**   ☐ **False**

4 "Tracy, what is this rumor I keep hearing about you?", Patti asked. Several people in the youth group were whispering about Tracy having been drunk at last Friday night's football game. She wasn't, but a lot of people were convinced she was.

How could this rumor affect Tracy? _____

What should Tracy do? _____

5 Mary's mouth has done all the actions described below. Choose the worst three and mark them with an **X**. Choose the best three and mark with a "happy face" (☺)

_____ Said something that hurt her best friend.
_____ Used foul language when she spilled Coke on her new outfit.
_____ Lied to her father.
_____ Gossiped about a friend at church.
_____ Thanked her mom for giving her a ride to school.

_____ Put down another person by calling her a dirty name.
_____ Said a comforting word to her grandfather.
_____ Told a dirty joke.
_____ Talked to her school counselor about a math class.
_____ Yelled at her brother.
_____ Boasted about herself.

_____ Witnessed to a friend
_____ Said "I love you" to her father.
_____ Lied to a friend.
_____ Gave a book report in English class.

6 Summarize **James 3:2-8** in twenty words or less.

_____

_____

_____

BIG MOUTH

Topic: Language: Taming the tongue

Purpose of this Session:

Since the time of Adam and Eve, the human race has had difficulty controlling its tongue, but only recently have young people been exposed so frequently to such rough language and inappropriate speech. Teen movies starring celebrities using foul language, gossip and viciously cutting remarks are being shown as examples of normal ways of speaking. This TalkSheet will help you discuss the relationship between the Christian faith and the words we say.

To Introduce the Session:

Play the game "Love Target". The group sits in a circle with one person in the middle, the bull's-eye. The students in the circle try to say as many nice things as possible about the one in the middle in two minutes. If you have enough students to form two groups, you could have them compete for points.

After the game, ask the group why it is so difficult to say nice things to each other on a normal day-to-day basis. It seems most of the time we have to endure put-downs, gossip, slams, foul language and rude comments from each other. Let's talk about talk; how what we say to each other makes a big difference in our lives.

Another way to introduce this TalkSheet is to play "The Gossip Game", in which the first student in the circle whispers a Bible verse into the ear of the second, and so on, around the circle. The object is to see if the last person in the circle gets the message in its original form. Usually the verse gets quite distorted. With two teams, you can have them compete for speed and accuracy.

The Discussion:

Item #1: For a fun opening exercise, have the students share some of their favorite slang expressions and explain them. Ask if they know how the expression got started. Be certain they refrain from off-color remarks. You might wish to start by sharing slang from your own teen years, such as "Groovy", "Boss", etc.

Item #2: Ask the group to share their experiences. Point out how easy it is to get into trouble with what we say.

Item #3: Ask for opinions on this question. Chances are you will hear a wide difference. Times have changed. It wasn't long ago that using a "swear word", now common in everyday speech, was considered a sin. There were certain words forbidden on radio and television, but this is no longer true.

What about Christians? Do we side with the popular custom and use "foul", "off-color" or "obscene" language? Is "cussing" ever appropriate? Discuss these questions with your group and ask for suggestions for other, better ways to express themselves in situations where foul language might be used. If you want to introduce scripture here, have someone read Exodus 20:7 and Ephesians 4:29-32. Discuss the pertinence of these Bible verses.

Item #4: Use this "Tension Getter" to discuss gossip. Have them answer the questions on their TalkSheet and ask if they have ever been in a situation like this themselves. How do rumors like this get started, when they are not true? Why is it we are always so eager to spread bad news about others? What should we do when we hear something bad about another? There is an old saying, "A tongue three inches long can kill a man six feet tall." Is that saying true?

Item #5: Ask the students to share their choices and give reasons why.

Item #6: Divide the students into small groups and ask for a consensus of their summaries. Talk about how easy it is to get into trouble by speaking carelessly, without thinking of the consequences. Ask them to contribute ways to avoid this kind of trouble.

To Close the Session:

Summarize the major points made in the session. Help the students see words are not neutral. Blaise Pascal once said, "Cold words freeze people and hot words scorch them, bitter words make them bitter and wrathful words make them wrathful." Conversely, kind and thoughtful words do wonders. Christians should be generous with them.

Many times we utter words we then wish were attached to a rope so we could pull them back inside. We can't. Encourage the students to think before they curse a teacher, say something hurtful to a parent, or gossip about a friend.

Outside Activities:

Ask the group to watch specific television shows and to count how many times foul language is used. The same can be done for movies. Discuss the results the next week.

PARENTS ARE PEOPLE, TOO

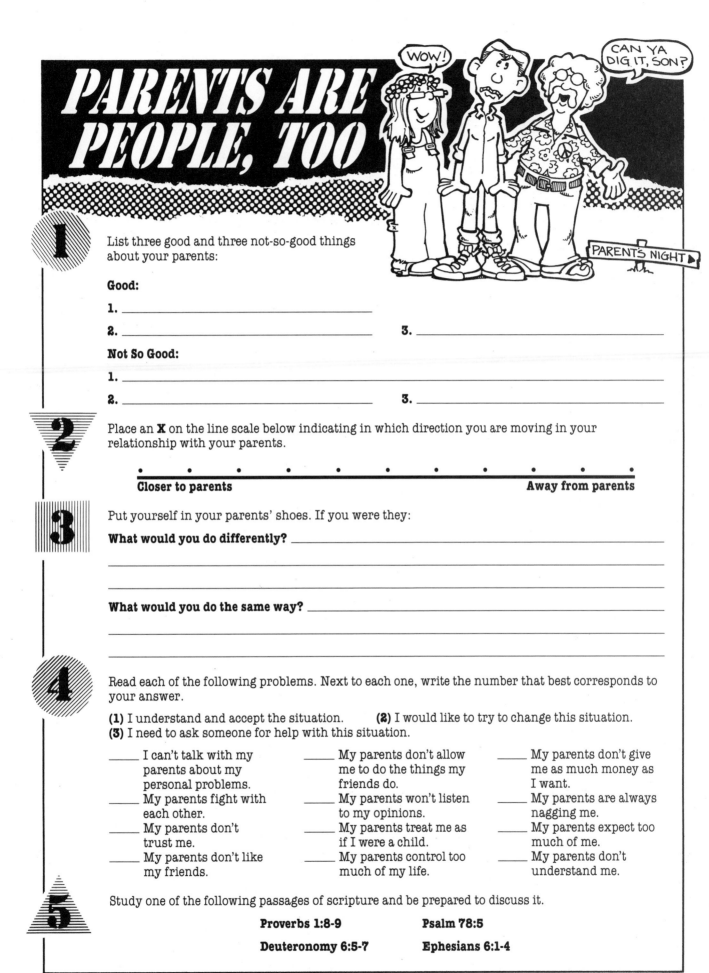

1 List three good and three not-so-good things about your parents:

Good:

1. _____

2. _____   3. _____

Not So Good:

1. _____

2. _____   3. _____

2 Place an **X** on the line scale below indicating in which direction you are moving in your relationship with your parents.

•   •   •   •   •   •   •   •   •   •   •

Closer to parents   **Away from parents**

3 Put yourself in your parents' shoes. If you were they:

What would you do differently? _____
_____
_____

What would you do the same way? _____
_____
_____

4 Read each of the following problems. Next to each one, write the number that best corresponds to your answer.

(1) I understand and accept the situation.   **(2)** I would like to try to change this situation.
(3) I need to ask someone for help with this situation.

_____ I can't talk with my parents about my personal problems.
_____ My parents fight with each other.
_____ My parents don't trust me.
_____ My parents don't like my friends.

_____ My parents don't allow me to do the things my friends do.
_____ My parents won't listen to my opinions.
_____ My parents treat me as if I were a child.
_____ My parents control too much of my life.

_____ My parents don't give me as much money as I want.
_____ My parents are always nagging me.
_____ My parents expect too much of me.
_____ My parents don't understand me.

5 Study one of the following passages of scripture and be prepared to discuss it.

Proverbs 1:8-9   Psalm 78:5

Deuteronomy 6:5-7   Ephesians 6:1-4

PARENTS ARE PEOPLE, TOO

Topic: Parent-teen Relationships

Purpose of this Session:

As children become adolescents, they begin to establish an identity of their own. They begin to separate themselves from their parents and to become independent. This always causes a certain amount of difficulty in the home. To the parents, the teenager seems rebellious and distant. To the teenager, the parents seem hopelessly old-fashioned and overly strict. This TalkSheet is to help you discuss parent-teen relationships with your students in a constructive and positive manner.

To Introduce the Topic:

Have the group role-play a few situations that involve parents and teenagers. For example, ask one to play the role of the parent and another the part of the teenager who wants to "go out" with some friends for the evening. The problem is that the teenager is "on restriction" for getting home fifteen minutes late the previous weekend. The teenager's "role" is to convince the "parent" he/she should be allowed to go. The "parent" should respond the way they think most parents would.

The Discussion:

Item #1: Make a master list of the bad and good characteristics of parents and display it. If your students are typical, they will find it easier to name faults than good qualities. Help them arrive at a more balanced viewpoint. You might turn this around and ask for good and bad things about themselves, from the parents' standpoint. Young people are learning their parents aren't perfect, but they need to realize they have their own imperfections as well.

Item #2: Ask for volunteers to talk about the status of their relationship with their parents. Once they have shared, ask them to think of ways they can improve their relationships with their parents.

Item #3: This exercise encourages young people to see things from their parents point of view. Have volunteers share their responses to the two questions — what they would do the same way and what they would do differently. Then ask them to give their reasons.

Item #4: Talk about each of these problem areas and watch for the ones where the most frequent response is "Try to change". With these, stop and ask the students how best the change could be brought about. For instance, how would they change a situation in which their parents don't trust them? What are some steps they can take to establish trust?

Some students will indicate they need help with problems. Let them know who is available and make certain they get the help they need from yourself, your pastor, other church parents or concerned adults, or a qualified counselor. Don't assume those with problems are getting help. They probably are not. You can perform a great minstry in their lives by referring them to responsible help.

Item #5: Ask the students to read these passages and to discuss them one at a time. Discuss ways these scriptures can be put into practice in parent-teen relationships.

To Close the Session:

Your youth group needs to be encouraged to hang in there with their parents. Keep your closing comments upbeat and positive. Here are a few points you can make:

Parents want the best for their children. They have invested a lot in their children's lives and care a great deal about them. Parents may not be perfect, but they are the only ones they have. God gave our parents to us and we need to be thankful for them.

They need to communicate with their parents and spend time with them. They should not always try to avoid them. They need to make an effort to find ways of opening up communication at home.

They need to attempt to see things from their parents' point of view. Parents are under a lot of pressure, just as the students are. There may be ways they can help take some of the pressure off the parents, which will only make life better for them.

Remember that God has commanded us to honor and obey our parents, even when they seem to be wrong (Exodus 20:12). This is one of the Ten Comandments and is irrevocable. But it also comes with a promise. We won't regret "hanging in there" with our parents through the teen years. It's always amazing when you become an adult yourself, how smart and wise our parents suddenly become.

It would be appropriate to close with a prayer for everyone's parents.

Outside Activities:

1. Have your students write a letter to their parents. They should include several words of appreciation and an "I love you". Some have difficulty telling their parents they love them. A letter can make this easier.

2. Schedule another meeting or a weekend retreat, including the students' parents. Role play a situation together, similar to the one described earlier, only have the parents play the parts of the teenagers and the teens the parents. Play games together, have discussions together and encourage parents and teens to discuss some of the issues raised in this TalkSheet.

YOU MAKE ME SO MAD

1 List three things that make you angry.

a. _____

b. _____

c. _____

2 Complete the sentence: "When I get angry, I _____

_____

_____."

3 What do you think?

	YES	NO
a. Everyone has feelings of anger.	☐	☐
b. A person can express their anger either in a positive or negative way.	☐	☐
c. I have a right to get angry when someone hurts me.	☐	☐
d. I feel uncomfortable expressing my anger.	☐	☐
e. A person should deal with their anger as soon as possible.	☐	☐

	YES	NO
f. People who lose their temper are showing their immaturity.	☐	☐
g. Hiding one's anger is the Christian thing to do.	☐	☐
h. Anger is a sin.	☐	☐
i. Christians should express anger differently from non-Christians.	☐	☐

4 For each of the following situations, write out a short response stating how you would honestly handle it.

SITUATION	RESPONSE
Someone calls you a name.	_____
Your parents blame you for something you didn't do.	_____
Someone steals a book from your locker at school.	_____
You are angry with yourself.	_____

5 Read each of the Bible verses below and then complete the sentences using what you learned from the Bible passage.

Proverbs 14:17   When I am angry, I _____

Proverbs 15:1   When I speak, I _____

Proverbs 29:11   I can control my anger by _____

Ephesians 4:26   If I am angry I _____

101

YOU MAKE ME SO MAD

Topic: Anger

Purpose of this Session:

Anger is a difficult emotion for most people to handle, especially teenagers. It is a negative emotion that can tear relationships apart and cause many other problems. There is a proverb that says, "Anger, like fire, finally dies out — but not before it leaves a path of destruction." Young people experience anger frequently as they are discovering the world is not as ideal as they would like for it to be. But they haven't yet learned how to handle this anger. This TalkSheet gives your group a chance to look at anger and decide how a Christian can handle it.

To Introduce the Topic:

Ask one of your young people who can do a little acting to help you introduce this session on anger. Discuss the plot with your "actor" beforehand. Before your meeting has even begun, have him or her "bug" you. During the opening of the meeting, the music, the announcements, the games, etc., have him or her heckle you unmercifully, literally disturbing the meeting. Right before you start a fake discussion, act as if you cannot take it anymore and blow up. Pretend to be very angry and lose control. Yell at your actor to get out and never come back. When he or she storms out, let the group in on the plot and tell them the subject of the discussion will be "anger".

The Discussion:

Item #1: Make a list of all the things that make your students angry. You may want to talk about the term "make you" and explain to them nothing really "makes us" mad. We are in control of our reactions and we *choose* to be angry in response to an action.

Item #2: Have the group share their completed sentences. A good follow-up question is to ask how their parents handle anger. In most cases, there are similarities between how anger is handled by parents and their offspring.

Item #3: Many young people have difficulty expressing anger. They either keep it inside themselves or let it out in inappropriate and destructive ways. Often they feel anger is a sin. It is not. It is a feeling, an emotion. Christ told us to be angry but not to sin. The anger is not the problem. It is what we do with it that counts. Communicate to the students through a discussion of these statements that anger is a normal feeling all of us have. What each of us needs to learn is appropriate ways to handle that anger.

Item #4: This exercise, along with #5, gives you the chance to examine appropriate and inappropriate ways to handle anger. Let different students share their responses to the situations. A good follow-up question is to determine if the responses suggested are "Christian" or not. Have them explain the reasons.

Item #5: These scriptures all focus on anger in different ways. Have the students complete the sentences and talk about what they learned from each of the verses.

To Close the Session:

Here's a good quote from Norman Vincent Peale: "Next time you feel the surge of anger, say to yourself, 'Is this really worth what it's going to do to me and another, emotionally? I will make a fool of myself. I may hurt someone I love, or I might lose a friend. Practice realizing it is not worth it to get so worked up over things and always remember the words of Seneca who said, 'The greatest cure for anger is delay.'"

Challenge your group members to "delay" expressing anger until they have had a chance to cool off. Then, they should express their anger in a very positive and constructive way. If they are still having trouble understanding how to handle their anger, have them role-play situations and alternative responses. Assure them their angry feelings are not sinful. It is how they respond to those feelings that is important.

Outside Activities:

1. Have the students search for newspaper articles during the week that illustrate anger. Debrief the articles they find by talking about why there is so much anger in our world and how they can be Christian peacemakers.

2. Ask several students to create a bulletin board or poster related to anger. Let them share what they learned from the experience.

3. Have the group members bring in a rock song whose lyrics express anger and rebellion. Play the song, then talk about why the anger was there and what could be done about it.

The Devil Made Me Do It

1 I am tempted to do things I know are wrong:
(choose one)

_____ More than most people

_____ About the same as most people

_____ Less then most people

2 When you are tempted to do something you know is wrong, what do you do? (place an **X** on the line scale)

◆　◆　◆　◆　◆　◆　◆　◆　◆　◆　◆

I usually give in   **I usually resist**

3 Imagine you are invited to go to a party where you might be tempted to sin. **What would you do?** (check one)

☐ I would not go

☐ I would take my chances and go

☐ I would ask my parents for advice

☐ I would go but I would not let myself be tempted

☐ I would go with another Christian friend

4 Complete the following sentences:

If I were to find a pornographic magazine, I would _____

_____

If I were tempted to cheat on a test, I would _____

_____

If I felt my parents were being unfair to me, I would _____

_____

If my friends decided to do something wrong, I would _____

_____

When I give in to temptation, I feel _____

_____

5 If someone were to ask you, "How can you overcome temptation?", what would you answer? Use these scriptures for ideas: **1 Corinthians 10:13　Psalm 119:11　James 4:7　John 16:33　Luke 22:46**

_____

_____

_____

_____

_____

_____

Date Used: _____

Group: _____

THE DEVIL MADE ME DO IT

Topic: Temptation

Purpose of this Session:

Pearl S. Buck once wrote, "Youth is the age of temptation." Temptation is a large part of an adolescent's life. Young people are frustrated because even though they want to live the Christian life, they find it very difficult to do. They are always yielding to temptation and then suffer with guilt as a result. This TalkSheet will help the students have a better understanding of temptation and how to deal with it.

To Introduce the Topic:

Ask each person to imagine the devil is sitting on one of their shoulders and an angel on the other. They are both trying to influence them to do something. What is it that they are trying to get them to do? Have the students describe their biggest temptations.

It would be fun to start this discussion by having the above acted out — let one person be the "victim", and two others take the parts of the devil and the angel, trying to be very persuasive. Give them a "scenario", such as "The person just saw a man accidentally drop a ten-dollar bill. What should he do now?" The devil tries to convince him to keep it and the angel insists it be returned to the owner.

The Discussion:

Item #1: Ask the students to share these responses. They majority may choose "more than most" or "the same as most". If anyone chooses "less than most", ask if they are ever tempted to lie.

This is a good place to make the point that temptation is a part of life and is not a sin. Playing with temptation invites sin. Fulton Sheen put it this way: "You are not tempted because you are evil; you are tempted because you are human."

Item #2: Some may feel comfortable sharing their answers to this one, but others may not. Do not force them to share. If someone says they usually give in, ask them why they think this happens. If someone says they usually resist, ask how they deal with temptation.

Item #3: Ask the group to decide as a unit what they think is the best answer.

Item #4: These incomplete sentences will give the students an opportunity to practice what they could do in tempting situations while in the security of the group environment. Ask them to volunteer their answers and discuss each one. The last item deals with feelings. Help them understand they don't have to carry around feelings of guilt or depression. When we yield to temptation and fall into sin, Jesus is there to pick us up and to forgive us. If we ask Jesus for help the next time, He will give us more strength to resist.

Item #5: Let the students work on these in small groups of two or three. Have them write out what they would say to someone who wanted to know how to overcome temptation, based upon these scripture passages. Let each group read their answers and ask everyone if they think these ideas from the Bible will work for them.

To Close the Session:

Young people need to know temptation is a normal part of growing up. They also need to know God has given them free will. The choice is theirs and the choices they make today will affect them in the future. Help them realize temptation will always be with them and that Satan will usually tempt them wherever they are most vulnerable. The only way they can resist is to stay close to Christ, who will give them the strength to do the right thing.

Temptation always makes sin look very attractive. It's similar to a television commercial, always putting the product (i.e., sinful behavior) in the best light. But when you actually "buy" the product, you discover you have been deceived and you are left feeling disappointed. Remember God knows what is best for us. Satan wants to destroy us and make our lives miserable. God wants us to get the most out of life, not the other way around.

Outside Activities:

Have the group search the scriptures for examples of temptation and how Biblical characters dealt with it.

What, Me Worry?

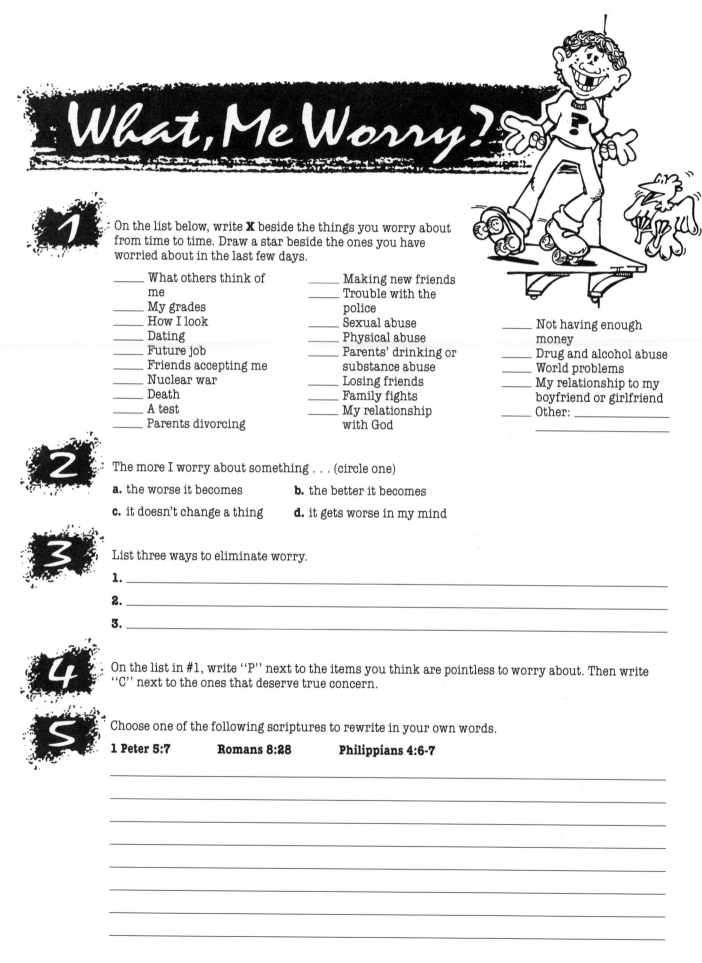

1 On the list below, write **X** beside the things you worry about from time to time. Draw a star beside the ones you have worried about in the last few days.

_____ What others think of me
_____ My grades
_____ How I look
_____ Dating
_____ Future job
_____ Friends accepting me
_____ Nuclear war
_____ Death
_____ A test
_____ Parents divorcing

_____ Making new friends
_____ Trouble with the police
_____ Sexual abuse
_____ Physical abuse
_____ Parents' drinking or substance abuse
_____ Losing friends
_____ Family fights
_____ My relationship with God

_____ Not having enough money
_____ Drug and alcohol abuse
_____ World problems
_____ My relationship to my boyfriend or girlfriend
_____ Other: _____
_____

2 The more I worry about something . . . (circle one)

a. the worse it becomes
b. the better it becomes
c. it doesn't change a thing
d. it gets worse in my mind

3 List three ways to eliminate worry.

1. _____
2. _____
3. _____

4 On the list in #1, write "P" next to the items you think are pointless to worry about. Then write "C" next to the ones that deserve true concern.

5 Choose one of the following scriptures to rewrite in your own words.

1 Peter 5:7   **Romans 8:28**   **Philippians 4:6-7**

_____
_____
_____
_____
_____
_____
_____
_____

Date Used: _____

Group: _____

WHAT, ME WORRY?

Topic: Worry

Purpose of this Session:

Today's young people function under a great deal of stress. They have a lot to worry about, but they lack the experience and maturity to deal with these worries in a constructive way. This TalkSheet will help your students talk about their worries in a supportive and caring atmosphere.

To Introduce the Session:

A fun way to begin is to play "Worries Charade". Choose a person, or yourself, to mime, silently, the different worries you have pre-selected and written down. The rest of the group tries to guess which worry the actor is portraying. Keep the worries humorous, such as body odor, pimple on nose, flunking a test, forgetting your date's name, not knowing how to kiss, can't get to sleep, going to the dentist, passing gas, etc.

Another humorous introduction to this session is to read a portion of the article "How to Worry" on page 87 of the book *Teenage Romance: or How to Die of Embarrassment* by Delia Aphron (Viking Press, 1981).

The Discussion:

Item #1: Begin by talking about things that worried you as a teenager. Then let the students share what things worry them the most. Act as moderator and listen to their concerns. You will gain valuable insight into their lives.

Item #2: The students will probably find logical reasons why each answer could be correct. Explain that worrying about something usually doesn't change it.

Item #3: Talk about different solutions to the problem of worrying. List others on the board.

Item #4: Ask the students to name the "worries" they think are pointless and those which deserve concern. Define the difference between the kind of worry that changes nothing and creative concern which motivates change. They need to see how worrying generates negative energy concentrated only in the problem itself. Creative concern uses positive energy to find a solution.

Item #5: After studying the scriptures together, ask the students to memorize one of them. They can repeat the scripture to themselves the next time they begin to worry.

To Close the Session:

The English word "worry" comes from the old German word *wurgen*, meaning "to choke". Worry is mental strangulation. It can kill.

It is normal and healthy to have worries, but it is destructive, self-defeating and useless to worry about things over which you have no control. If you can control an outcome of a "worry", then you can do something about it in a positive way.

Help them understand Christians need not worry about what has happened in the past, nor about the future. Both are in God's hands. We are forgiven the past and God is in control of the future. Jesus came to give us inner peace and a positive outlook on life. Jesus says to us, "Do not worry, little flock" (Matthew 6).

The saints of the church prayed this prayer: "God grant me the serenity to accept the things I cannot change, courage to change the things I can, and wisdom to know the difference."

Tell your group one of the best ways to get rid of worry is to talk about it with someone else. Let them know you are available to listen and to help. Sometimes the only thing young people need is the opportunity to dump some of their worries on someone else.

Outside Activities:

1. The best way to forget your troubles is to help someone else. Plan a Christian service project such as reading stories to patients in a children's hospital, visiting a retirement home or helping for a day in a rescue mission.

2. Ask the students to interview adults in the church about their worries. Have them compare the worries of adults with the worries of teenagers.

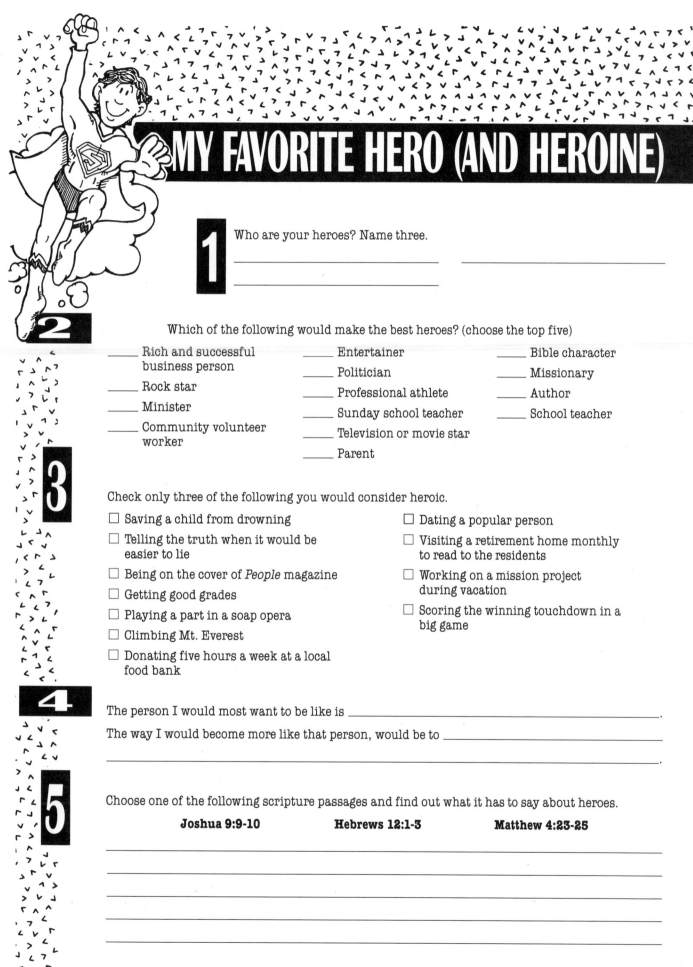

MY FAVORITE HERO (AND HEROINE)

1 Who are your heroes? Name three.

_____   _____
_____

2 Which of the following would make the best heroes? (choose the top five)

_____ Rich and successful business person
_____ Rock star
_____ Minister
_____ Community volunteer worker

_____ Entertainer
_____ Politician
_____ Professional athlete
_____ Sunday school teacher
_____ Television or movie star
_____ Parent

_____ Bible character
_____ Missionary
_____ Author
_____ School teacher

3 Check only three of the following you would consider heroic.

☐ Saving a child from drowning
☐ Telling the truth when it would be easier to lie
☐ Being on the cover of _People_ magazine
☐ Getting good grades
☐ Playing a part in a soap opera
☐ Climbing Mt. Everest
☐ Donating five hours a week at a local food bank

☐ Dating a popular person
☐ Visiting a retirement home monthly to read to the residents
☐ Working on a mission project during vacation
☐ Scoring the winning touchdown in a big game

4 The person I would most want to be like is _____.

The way I would become more like that person, would be to _____

_____.

5 Choose one of the following scripture passages and find out what it has to say about heroes.

Joshua 9:9-10   **Hebrews 12:1-3**   **Matthew 4:23-25**

_____
_____
_____
_____
_____

Date Used: _____

Group: _____

MY FAVORITE HERO (AND HEROINE)

Topic: Heroes

Purpose of this Session:

Far too many of today's heroes and heroines are creations of the media. They are celebrities shaped by television, movies and videos. They range from rock stars to television personalities. They are not the role models we want our young people to emulate. This TalkSheet will help your group discuss what a hero actually should be.

To Introduce the Session:

For a wildly humorous introduction: discuss the "plot" beforehand with three of the students, one of whom plays the "villian" and the other, the "victim". In the opening "scene", the "villian" is about to kill the "heroine" and suddenly "Superman", wearing a rented costume, leaps into the room and the heroine cries out, "My hero!" A good "Superman" skit can be found in the book *The Greatest Skits on Earth* by Rice and Yaconelli (Zondervan, 1986).

A less dramatic way to start this session would be to display several popular news and sports magazines that feature individuals on their covers. Ask the students to rate the famous people according to their "hero potential".

The Discussion:

Item #1: Ask the group to name their heroes and heroines. See how many are the same ones. Have the students tell why they were chosen. If they try to spiritualize this too much (by naming Jesus Christ or the apostle Paul, etc.) limit the answers to present-day human beings.

Item #2: Try to obtain a group consensus on this item. Ask "What is the difference between a hero and a celebrity?" Heroes do heroic things. They are worthy of admiration even if they are not well-known. Celebrities are media creations. They are people who are famous not necessarily because of anything worthy they have achieved, but sometimes just because they are notorious. The emphasis on celebrities has detracted from our sense of right and wrong because celebrity stature is often achieved by immoral people.

Item #3: As responses are shared to this question, point out heroic deeds do not always bring fame. Fame has very little to do with that which is truly heroic or morally correct.

Item #4: Ask the students to share the name of their choice. Many will choose Jesus or their parents. This is a good time to talk about who they would like as their life's model — Jesus and parents are very good choices as role models. Ask them to think of things they can do to pattern their lives after those they admire.

Another good point to make is that the best way to identify with our heroes is to *do what they do*. Most young people identify with their heroes not by doing what they do but by wearing a T-shirt with their hero's picture on it or trying to emulate the way their hero dresses. Those are superficial ways. If you admire a great musician, the thing to do is work hard to become a better musician yourself. We identify with Christ not so much by wearing a Christian T-shirt, but by imitating Christ's humility, His concern for others, His love of God, etc.

Item #5: Let the students share their discoveries from these scripture passages. You may also want to read Hebrews 11, which discusses heroes and heroines of the Christian faith.

To Close the Session:

Everyone needs a hero, but we should choose our heroes carefully. The apostle Paul said "Imitate me". He wasn't boasting. He was saying, "I'll be your hero. You need a hero who does what Jesus wants him to do. Imitate me as I imitate Christ." (Phil. 3:17) Don't model yourself after anyone who does not reflect the values and high standards of the Christian faith.

Challenge your young people not only to choose their heroes carefully but also to strive to do the heroic deed. Many may believe they are "nobodies", but encourage them to believe they can do great things for the kingdom of God. "I can do all things through Christ who gives me strength", wrote Paul (Phil. 4:13). Let the group know there are younger Christians looking up to them.

Outside Activities:

1. Have the students ask their parents who their heroes and heroines were when they were growing up.

2. Assign a written report about a hero or heroine of their choosing.

I AIN'T GOT NOBODY

1 List three of your best friends and give one reason why they are such good friends.

FRIEND

1. _____
2. _____
3. _____

REASON

1. _____
2. _____
3. _____

2 Here's your chance to "buy the perfect friend". You have 25 cents to spend. **How will you spend it?**

Each of these qualities costs 6 cents:
- ○ Has lots of money
- ○ Very popular
- ○ Very intelligent
- ○ Strong Christian
- ○ Kind and considerate

Each of these qualities costs 5 cents:
- ○ Good looking
- ○ Good conversationalist
- ○ Outgoing personality
- ○ Sense of humor
- ○ High moral standards

Each of these qualities costs 4 cents:
- ○ Has a car
- ○ Has the right clothes
- ○ Has a lot of time
- ○ Extremely loyal
- ○ Very dependable

Each of these qualities costs 3 cents:
- ○ Likes the same things you do
- ○ Honest
- ○ Good listener
- ○ Very generous

Each of these qualities costs 2 cents:
- ○ Has nice house
- ○ Has sex appeal
- ○ Has nice parents
- ○ Same age as you

Each of these qualities costs 1 cent:
- ○ Has athletic ability
- ○ Lives close to your house
- ○ Has no other friends
- ○ Very talented

3 What do you think?

	YES	NO
a. I feel I choose the right kind of friends.	☐	☐
b. I do not like the friends I now have.	☐	☐
c. I think a best friend should be a Christian.	☐	☐
d. My friends influence me in negative ways more than I influence them in positive ways.	☐	☐
e. I get along very well with my friends.	☐	☐

	YES	NO
f. I have a difficult time making friends.	☐	☐
g. I believe my friends talk about me behind my back.	☐	☐
h. I wish I had a best friend.	☐	☐
i. My parents don't like my friends.	☐	☐
j. I wish I could find some new friends.	☐	☐

4 Read **Colossians 3:12-14**. What are some characteristics of friendship found in this scripture?

_____

_____

_____

Date Used: _____

Group: _____

I AIN'T GOT NOBODY

Topic: Friendship

Purpose of this Session:

Having friends is the lifeblood of adolescence. A big issue with any youth group is friends — how to get them, keep them, get rid of them and be one of them. This TalkSheet will help your group discuss friendship from a Christian perspective.

To Introduce the Topic:

Read several "help wanted" ads to the students, then have them write a "want ad" seeking a friend. Ask for volunteers to share their "Friend Wanted" ads with the rest of the group. You will be surprised how creative they can be.

If you have access to a telephone amplifier and a telephone near the meeting room, have a student telephone a friend during the meeting attempting to get their friend to do something slightly unreasonable, such as go on a blind date, come over and change a diaper on a baby the student is supposedly baby-sitting, bring over their homework paper to copy, etc. They have three minutes to convince their friend to do the chosen task. This could be a lot of fun and a good introduction into a discussion of friendship as well.

The Discussion:

Item #1: Ask volunteers to describe some of their friends and why they are good friends. Not everyone will want to mention their friends' names.

Item #2: Ask several students to describe the friend they "bought" for a quarter. Concentrate the discussion on which qualities are truly important in a friendship. Tell the group they may add any characteristics not on the list, and those characteristics are free.

Item #3: Discuss these items one by one. Do not force sharing. On items such as "My parents don't like my friends", ask the group why this might be true and what they think can be done to remedy the situation.

A good general question here would be "What did you learn from these statements?" Some will say they realize they would like to have more friends. Encourage them to befriend someone not in their immediate circle. Talk about the obstacles sometimes encountered when trying to make friends outside their special clique.

Item #4: In this passage, there are eight characteristics of friendship: compassion, kindness, humility, gentleness, patience, bearing, forgiving and loving. Emphasize how important it is not to think of these traits as things to be expected from a friend, but as qualities that will make them a good friend to others.

To Close the Session:

Read Proverbs 18:24: "A good friend shows himself friendly." In other words, in order to *have* good friends, we must be a good friend. Friendships rarely happen by accident. They need mutual consideration and effort.

Alan Loy McGinnis, in his gook *The Friendship Factor* lists five important steps to getting and keeping good friends: (1) Give your friendships top priority. Don't take them for granted. (2) Cultivate transparency. Be open and honest with your friends. (3) Let your friends know they mean a lot to you. Affirm your friends and tell them you appreciate their friendship. (4) Learn the gestures of love. In other words, do things for your friends unselfishly. Put your friendship into action. (5) Create space in your relationship. Don't try to control the other person. Allow them to be themselves. Accept the way they are.

Let the students know Christ wants them to have friends. Jesus Himself had friends, a close group of men and women with whom He spent a lot of time. He frequently taught about how to be a good friend and neighbor to others and how to relate to people in a positive way.

Jesus also wants to be our friend. He is a friend "who sticks closer than a brother". If we have Christ as our friend, we will have many other friends who also know Christ. That is what the youth group and the church is all about: The Body of Christ.

Close with a prayer asking that Christ draw everyone in the youth group closer to each other as friends, united in Him.

Outside Activities:

1. Have the group members pretend they are applying for a job as "friend". As part of the application, they must list all their qualifications for being a friend.

2. Have the group study the Biblical friendships of David and Jonathan (I Samuel 18, 19) and Jesus and Lazarus (John 11) to discover why they were such good friends.

3. Ask the students each to try and find a new friend sometime during the next month.